TRUMP: THE DESTINY OF GOD'S AMERICA

TRUMP: THE DESTINY OF GOD'S AMERICA

THE GREAT AWAKENING AND BATTLE FOR OUR COUNTRY'S FUTURE

JEFF JANSEN

CONTENTS

FOREWORD I

When Jeff Jansen told me about George Washington's vision and the firsthand account that was placed in the Library of Congress, I wanted to know more. Then, when he told me two of the three perils Washington recorded had already happened, I became more interested. My interest peaked when I found out that one of the two 2020 Presidential candidates was mentioned by name! When the first President of the United States has a vision from God, as an investigative reporter of the supernatural, I am all ears!

What President George Washington saw in 1777 looks like something that could happen right NOW! I feel very strongly the devil is trying to speed up end-time events. Why? Because God wants more people saved! And the best prophets I know have seen the Global Glory starting this year. This will be different than any outpouring in history. It will be world-wide and with 100 times more power than any generation has ever seen. Jesus said in John 14:12, "...he who believes in Me will do the works that I do also. And he will do GREATER WORKS than these...". It will not be just a few superstars but will be those that have made Jesus Savior and Lord! Note the word "Lord". This outpouring will be seen, felt and heard. The visible Glory of God will be visibly seen by everyone in an auditorium, believers and nonbelievers alike. They will see the same clouds that the Jewish people saw over Moses and Mount Sinai in the desert for forty years!

The common sign of *this* awakening will be deep repentance.

If the devil can speed up end-time events, then fewer will be saved. That is his diabolical strategy. I believe the ONLY thing to delay this strategy is deep repentance for sin and voting for the President that God has chosen! Again, note the word "vote". I pray you read this book and see the gravity of the times we are living in. As Mordecai told Queen Esther, a type of the end time church, in Esther 4:14(NLT)

"If you keep quiet at a time like this, you and your relatives will die. Who knows if perhaps you were made queen for just such a time as this?" Esther prayed, repented and fasted and changed the heart of the king.

Prayer, repentance and you voting the candidate of God's choice can give us more time to evangelize the world! But who is the Presidential candidate of God's choice?

God has always had three main areas that trigger judgement on a nation. These areas are His three 'deal breakers' according to the Bible!

1. The first is *child sacrifice* to appease false gods. The old false god was called "Baal." The new false God is called "Pleasure". In the United States, since 1973 (Roe

vs. Wade), over 60 million babies have been sacrificed on the altar to the god of 'Pleasure'. Less than one percent (0.8%) of those abortions have been due to health concerns for the mother!

2. The second sin that triggers destruction of a nation is to destroy the very foundation of marriage, which is between a man and a woman. Today, our children are being taught, as early as elementary school, that homosexuality is normal! The next generation has no chance...

3. The third sin that releases judgment on a nation is coming against the Jew and Israel.

"I will bless them who bless you
and curse him who curses you,
and in you all families of the earth
will be blessed." (Genesis 12:3)

Count the cost. REPENT, PRAY AND VOTE!

—SID ROTH
TV Show Host, *It's Supernatural!*

FOREWORD II

The DESTINY OF GOD'S AMERICA by best-selling author, Jeff Jansen is a mandate that must not be ignored.

Throughout history, nations and civilizations have risen and fallen. We see genuine deliverance only when leaders and the people cry out and return to God. The timing of the release of this book is telling and foretelling.

In 2020, America's battle with evil working to overtake good reaches epic proportions, and the shockwaves ripple around the world. Yet, there is a remnant holding fast to the truth. GOD is Sovereign.

"And hath made of one blood all nations of men for to dwell on all the face of the earth, and hath determined the times before appointed, and the bounds of their habitation; That they should seek the Lord, if haply they might feel after him, and find him, though he be not far from every one of us: For in him we live, and move, and have our being; as certain also of your own poets have said, For we are also his offspring" (Acts 17:26-28, KJV)

In America and around the world, human dignity, life, and procreation are at risk. Life is a civil right! From the womb to the tomb, we as human beings are one blood, one race. Only the blood of Christ is stronger. Donald John Trump, America's most Pro-Life President ever, understands this.

Donald J. Trump, the 45th President of The United States of America, said, "We all bleed the same..."

During the first presidential debate for the primaries of the 2016 election in America, I remember texting friends and saying, "Mr. Trump is like a bull in a china shop." Then God revealed this to me: "Yes, and bulls are beautiful and magnificent creatures, and china is fragile."

In the context of America's economy, the bull represents a strong economy. Even in the face of COVID-19 and the street riots of 2020, we must remember we entered this era with a strong economy, and the job rate for African Americans is the highest in recent history. And yes, the China issue is very fragile.

Since that time, America has elected a president who has not been afraid to pray in the White House. With the help of The Holy Spirit, many have rallied and returned to God.

THE DESTINY OF GOD'S AMERICA is a prophetic guidepost. With God's guidance, let us read on and lead on, continuing to shine the light of Christ.

—EVANGELIST ALVEDA C. KING
Civil Rights for The Unborn

INTRODUCTION
PROPHETIC PERSPECTIVE

I think we can all agree that we are in a defining moment in American history. Prophets played a significant role in Israel's history, and until this present day, the voice of the prophets has articulated God's word in perilous times. The prophets hear the voice of God and observe the world from His perspective. The divine conscience and pathos of God impinge upon the daily life of the prophet, awakening them to coming shifts of historical importance. This divine intrusion gradually translates into a message for the nations, a word written by the finger of God and delivered to the prophet. God's conscience illuminates the soul of the prophet, while his pathos empowers him with passion for the people. In his unique way, Abraham Heschel creatively envisioned the word and the event as a divine expression.

"They experienced the word as a living manifestation of God, and events in the world as effects of His activity. The given factor, whether the word or the event, was for them an expression of the divine."[1]

Heschel describes the prophetic event impressing itself on the prophet as a happening that springs exclusively from the will and initiative of God. The prophetic experience is more than an encounter; it is a sense of being overpowered by the word. He does not seize the moment; the moment seizes him. He has no option, and in Heschel's words, the word is violently, powerfully urged upon him.[2]

The Old Testament prophets stood alone, as one voice, on behalf of God. They are beholden to no man. Their ultimate allegiance is to God alone, not to the ruling powers. They stand in a solitary place to be a unique, unbiased voice speaking God's word as His chosen representative. Juxtaposed between God and the world, they become the conscience of the nation, providing an alternative perception that often opposes the king. Concerning the task of prophetic ministry, Walter Brueggemann finds the needle in the prophetic haystack when he wrote these words.

"The task of prophetic ministry is to nurture, nourish, and evoke a consciousness and perception alternative to the consciousness and perception of the dominant culture around us."[3]

The Lord has been clearly speaking to me through dreams and visions concerning the nature of what is happing in our nation in these present days. We are wrestling for the soul of America and fighting for her future. At stake is the potential loss of the founding core values that made our country great, and the blood spilled for its freedom. I've heard many preachers and prophets say that America is being judged for her evil activities and that God is punishing us now due to our national sins. I'm not advocating that America is exempt from consequences for actions and bad decisions we have made. I believe in the law of reaping and sowing that produce consequences for our actions.

The downward spiral into the darkness of immorality, rejection of God, despicable acts of violence, treacherous deeds of those in high positions, discrimination, abortion and injustice will get God's attention. The downward spiral has created a disconnect with the spiritual values that made America great. Yes, these things must be addressed and changed. This is not the America which we love.

This is part of the spiritual and political process of the cleansing and healing of America. We were founded as one nation under God, indivisible, which means never to be divided at this time or in the future. God loves this great nation, and as history makers, we are a nation which will make the necessary adjustments to return to God, and our core values. Though cataclysmic shifts are happening in this nation, we are living in times of a great awakening. I can assure you God is rejoicing over this nation that loves and acknowledges Him.

Since the Civil War, we have never lived in such a divisive time as these times. Once, it almost destroyed our nation. We will not let it happen again. As you read through the pages of this book, a prophetic picture of God's heart for this America will begin to manifest itself. It will be apparent that God has a covenant with us, and He will uphold His end of the bargain. If we remain faithful to our covenant with God, I guarantee we have a bright future while standing as one nation under God. *For united we stand, divided we fall.*

After Solomon dedicated the temple, the Lord appeared to him and gave him some warnings and promises. At night, the Lord appeared to Solomon and said: "I have heard your prayer and have chosen this place for myself as a temple for sacrifices." God followed up this word with warnings and promises.

The warnings are directed toward a nation. When Israel forsook God's law set before them, and had not obeyed His voice, God warned them, and in some cases, judged them harshly.

"When I shut up the heavens so that there is no rain, or command locusts to devour the land or send a plague among my people."

God's blessings and promises are reserved for a people and nation who will humble themselves, pray, seek His face, and obey His voice. As one, we stand on His word.

> "If my people, who are called by my name, will humble themselves and pray and seek my face and turn from their wicked ways, then I will hear from heaven, and I will forgive their sin and will heal their land." [4]

Eternity has entered the moment, and we respond in a doxological moment. "As it was in the beginning, is now, and will be forever." God, in his unchanging goodness, entered into time without compromising his eternal perfection. From the standpoint of eternity, God makes the "now" part of the "forever" and embeds the passing moment with eternal significance. We pray that the Lord will once again enter into time and heal our land.

We choose to be instruments of healing in the hands of a loving God.

We live in a moment of eternal significance. The future is ours, but now is the time for action. The words of Tony Evans are appropriate for these critical times in which we live.

"The future of our culture is in the hands of Christians because the cause of our cultural demise is innately spiritual. And if a problem is spiritual, its cure must be spiritual as well. If we Christians are going to help turn our nation to God, we must fall on our knees and our faces before God and pray. We must not only talk about prayer, but pray. Not only agree on the importance of prayer, but pray. Not only preach on the power of prayer, but pray. As Billy Graham once said, "To get our nation on its feet, we must get on our knees."

In the face of his nation's ongoing cultural demise, Nehemiah didn't sit down and write out a "Great Society" program for Jerusalem. He didn't propose a Jerusalem "New Deal." He fasted and prayed and sought God. As he did so, God revealed His strategy—and reversed years of deterioration in just 52 days. This is because prayer saves time." [5]

—JEFF JANSEN
Global Fire Ministries International

LAND OF THE FREE AND HOME OF THE BRAVE

America has made meaningful advancements in our lifespan. Many still remember when blacks and whites could not go to school together, women could not vote, there was no racial equality, and most children did not have an opportunity for a college education. The rates of disease were terrifying. We had not yet conquered polio. We had not yet found cures for many other maladies.

The progress we made is the foundation for a new American Dream. We can use the diversity, the strength, the commitment, and the genius of our country, all working together to make this country more significant than it is now.

Indeed, we face considerable obstacles to creating that dream. We must remain vigilant and determined not to allow anarchists and socialists to destroy what millions sacrificed to build over the last centuries.

I think the opportunities are there. It is essential that we not allow those opportunities to be ruined by present divisiveness.

The encroachment of dissension is one of the things that imperil the American Dream. We need to work together. It is essential we do what our forefathers and foremothers have always done, in adversity, they came together and emerged more durable than before. I think we can do that. We have done it during the time I have been alive, and I think we can do even more in the future.

Most Americans remember the sacrifices of citizens and soldiers over the past generations. Millions of them who worked, built, fought, and died for American democracy will not allow it to slip on their watch.

THE CHALLENGES BEFORE US

Newt Gingrich served as Speaker of the U.S. House of Representatives from 1995-1998. He was the first Republican to hold the office in 40 years. Gingrich stood tall and fought hard to maintain our freedom and counterattacked the deconstruction of our American heritage and values. This is from an article he recently wrote.

"This year, we are being challenged, once again, to be brave if we want to remain free. The events of the last few months have made it clear that if we are not brave (and therefore unwilling to stand and fight when necessary), then we will not be free for much longer. "Our American civilization is under assault from a variety of anti-American forces. They are anti-American because their goal is to replace America with a different system based on different values. They are anti-American because they refuse to obey the law, and they refuse to rely on the process of free speech and honest elections to change things.

"At a practical level, this anti-American force is assaulting our rights under the First Amendment. They are precisely the mob the Founding Fathers feared could topple our democratic republic. The videos of arrogant, dangerous mobs threatening people, while standing on their private property, are videos of an anti-American force seeking change through intimidation and coercion.

"The stated purpose of many of the organizations seeking to destroy traditional America is remarkably clear. The arrogance of ignorant ideologues lecturing the rest of us – holding our history in contempt, trying to destroy the memory of the great men and women who made America extraordinary – is a direct threat to the survival of our country.

"For too long, those of us who love America, deem it worthy of protecting, and believe it *must* be saved for the future of freedom on the planet have been quiet, reasonable, intimidated, and hiding.

"President Abraham Lincoln (the Great Emancipator despite all the lies told about him by the Left) captured the essence of this struggle over the nature of America in his address at Gettysburg in November 1863. Lincoln reminded his audience, "Now we are engaged in a great civil war, testing whether that nation or any nation so conceived and so dedicated, can long endure."

Today, I would replace "civil war" with "civic struggle," but the meaning and the threat is the same.

Lincoln went on to assert:

"It is for us the living, rather, to be dedicated here to the unfinished work which they who fought here have thus far so nobly advanced. It is rather for us to be here dedicated to the great task remaining before us—that from these honored dead we take increased devotion to that cause for which they gave the last full measure of devotion—that we here highly resolve that these dead shall not have died in vain—that this nation, under God, shall have a new birth of freedom—and that government of the people, by the people, for the people, shall not perish from the earth."

"It is time to reassert the rule of law, the spirit of America, and the potential of a genuine new birth of freedom. We must reject the rule of the mob and uphold government "of the people, by the people, and for the people."[1]

LAND OF THE FREE, HOME OF THE BRAVE

Lincoln called for all Americans to respond so that all those who died to preserve freedom in America shall not have died in vain. Francis Scott Key reminds us that freedom requires bravery. The final lines of the Star-Spangled Banner still ring true, more than ever.

> Praise the Power that hath made and preserved us a
> nation.
> Then conquer we must, when our cause it is just,
> And this be our motto: "In God is our trust."
> And the star-spangled banner in triumph shall wave
> O'er the land of the free and the home of the brave!

"There is a certain enthusiasm in liberty, that makes human nature rise above itself, in acts of bravery and heroism" (Alexander Hamilton). There are so many ways to display bravery. Sometimes, courage involves laying down your life for something bigger than yourself. Others exhibited bravery by giving up everything, for those they have never known, or for everyone they have ever loved, for something greater. There are times when bravery is nothing more than gritting your teeth, enduring the pain, resisting the temptation to give up, and hanging tight to the end to produce a better quality of life for the ones you love.

The bravest are surely those who have the clearest vision of what is before them, glory and danger alike and yet notwithstanding go out to meet it. Bravery and strength are like a magnet, drawing others to stand with them in the dark days of difficulty.

Courageous people do not necessarily have all the answers. Still, when challenged, something rises within, and with a deep conviction of soul, stimulated by bedrock faith, they press forward into the battle. Anyone who thinks bravery is about facing death without flinching is misunderstood. One sign of bravery is getting up each morning and putting one foot in front of the other, no matter how unpleasant and difficult the situation. These actions are typically photographed and labeled as signs of "bravery."

Facing life through the angst and agony of doing what is right takes courage. Refusing to bend in the face of danger, the fearless ones rise above their weaknesses and insecurities and embrace the challenge because of the love of family. It is God and country, even when nobody is looking. Courage is not listed as one of God's given virtues, but its value is exhibited in the exercise of strength in the hour of its most significant test.

Real Americans are patriotic and loyal people with a rock-solid core of dependability and love their moms, apple pie, and Jesus. They were raised to be fundamentally tough and physically present when the rubber meets the road. This toughness was forged in the furnace of affliction by mothers and fathers who sacrificed much for the next generation. They understood what it meant to be defenders of the faith and were devoted to the core values that made this nation great.

With confidence, I can say that America is the most astounding nation on the planet, beyond a shadow of a doubt. It was built on principles of freedom, rugged individualism, and self-sufficiency. No country has ever accumulated more power and wealth, abused it less, or used that power more to advance the human condition. Brave men and women sacrificed life and limb for a country where religious and social freedom fills the heart of every person fortunate enough to live in this beloved country.

Our history extends from the founding days of the Revolutionary War with General George Washington fighting for freedom at Valley Forge, to the 1860s when President Abraham Lincoln fought to end slavery. In Lincoln's Emancipation Proclamation, he audaciously affirmed that all men are free and equal in God's eyes and that a nation divided against itself will not stand. Those words became a light brightly shining in each generation.

FESTERING WOUNDS AND THE RESISTANCE

Even as America blossomed into the 20th Century, a leftwing socialistic radicalism, embedded in resentment, was festering beneath the surface, threatening to undermine democracy, first in the sixties and now again in 2020, probably more insidious than ever. A gnawing wound caused by irrational social justice warriors, the deep state of collusion and cronyism, and the compromised institutions of academia and the mainstream media created the resistance to the Great American Comeback.

Suppose we succumb to a Democratic victory in 2020. It will be nothing short of a big step toward full-blown socialism and increased economic pressures on the nation and a continuation of social conflict. If this happens, history will record in astonishment that the people who had the greatest to lose did the least to keep the freedoms that forged this country.

Radical Democrats are knocking at the door demanding the Green New Deal, socialized medicine, abortion on demand, open borders, abolishing the Electoral College, packing the Supreme Court with liberal judges, and an end to free speech. Our great nation would be fundamentally transformed beyond recognition.

Of all of his remarks, the Reagan Freedom Speech is perhaps his most iconic, as it not only shed light on the precarious nature of freedom but served as inspiration for generations to come. He delivered the famous address on Oct. 27, 1964, at the Republican National Convention, years before becoming President.

That speech catapulted him to political fame, paving the way for his path to the White House, and laying the foundation for his eventual presidential platform. However, the Reagan Freedom Speech was not political pandering or an attempt to seek party favor. The ideas and ideals he espoused were always manifest throughout his time in public office and after that. This is the crux of the Reagan Freedom Speech, also known as "A Time for Choosing":

"Freedom is never more than one generation away from extinction. We did not pass it to our children in the bloodstream. It must be fought for, protected and handed on for them to do the same, or one day we will spend our sunset years telling our children and our children's children what it was once like in the United States where men were free."[2]

We are at another crossroads similar to Raegan's first election. The truth is that the future of American freedom is connected to Donald Trump's reelection. It is time for every true American to act while standing for freedom.

The nation's Great Comeback, under President Donald Trump's leadership, has been amazing. During his first term, he dismantled the wall of socialistic policies and laws. The dismantling and rebuilding began with the 185 judges he appointed, continuing with the states' abortion bans, slow removal of Obama Care (affordable care act that was not so affordable), immigration reform and restrictions, ongoing cleansing of the justice system and the FBI, reducing taxes, introducing new education policies, and standing firm against the UN, and other international organizations.

He could have done more if it were not for the highly contentious and desperate efforts by the elites in academia, the media, and the Washington establishment to undermine and distort his achievements and halt his progress. The Americans who elected President Trump expect him to make good on his iconic call to "Make America Great Again," and he is making good on his promises.

The Deep State swamp is being drained, the economy is proliferating, and unemployment was in decline before Covid-19 hit our country. America's strength and standing as the world's dominant super-power are improving daily and will continue to do, as long as he is elected to a second term.

Meanwhile, Trump's opponents in Washington and the media are attempting to mock everything he does, only to spoil his election. The real America understands the challenges facing this nation and the role fake news plays in modern politics. Donald Trump tells the truth that the media and Washington elites do not want you to hear.

Hard-hitting questions require an answer to our country's demise. It is obvious that pride, greed, and power have obfuscated the truth, compelled men to do the unthinkable, including duplicitous deals with the most corrupt and destructive global leaders on earth. How did this happen in our country on our watch? How did the bankruptcy begin and who were the predators to whom "land of the free and home of the brave" fell victim?

Ye, this question pleads for an answer. Have we lost our hope? I do not want to linger too much longer on reviewing the past, but it is important before we focus on the present and future possibilities awaiting us. How we got here is not as important as how we rise above the mountain of deception and stack of disastrous decisions created by a socialist agenda. Is all hope lost? Gazing into the future, there is not a crystal ball that can magically answer the question. However, in this book, I will unveil a divine perspective coupled with prophetic insight through dreams and visions, leading us to renewed hope for an expected future.

We are living in the most seditious times, but also the most promising times! Seditious because of the incessant political scandals rising from Washington's evil swamp, most of us sick in the stomach because of the political roller coaster that never stops. The deep state and its progressive political cadre's relentless attacks against President Trump is wearisome. Couple with the negative barrage from the left we are subjected daily to, including the starry-eyed 2020 progressive presidential candidates promising an unattainable nirvana with free social goodies. Unfortunately, a liberal post-Christian community gullibly digs into their pocket full of lies, shenanigans, and empty promises. Or, because of their hatred of Trump, are willing to accept candidates who are a collection of ill-informed, unqualified, and deceiving politicians who, in previous times, would never be accepted, even by their own party?

Too many Americans pricked their finger on the spindle of a spinning wheel and fell asleep, totally unaware of the danger that lurks just around the corner. Others have succumbed to a host of occult connections, real evil influencers that could well destroy this country and make her irrelevant for the end times. Heaven is exposing the occult influences hidden, especially within Washington's deep state.

If the current direction of America is not quickly reversed, all hope will be lost. But I am a man of hope. My trust is in the Lord, and I believe our future shimmers like a finely cut diamond. This is not the fate of our Great America. From the beginning, God had a prophetic plan for the nation, starting with its founding fathers to the great men and women who will guide us into the future.

Unfortunately, the American dream has become the American nightmare. As a nation, we have gradually drifted from where our founding fathers started this great nation to a difficult but not impossible place to recover. Recent history reminds us that President Trump, a modern-day Cyrus-like figure, came to the Oval Office promising much and his first term delivered on that promise. He campaigned for the presidency, promising to return the power to the people by robbing the deep state of its ill-conceived influence. With the help of former FBI Director James Comey and John Brenan, the former head of the Central Intelligence Agency, the seen and unseen allies of the political elite have done everything possible to bring him down. He has fought hard and has many moments of success against liberal media's fake news, which daily spits out venomous attacks on our President. Despite these challenges, President Trump rebuilt America's economy and returned many jobs to America's heartland, jobs robbed by the likes of the Chinese communist. As God's chosen, he deserves our applause and another term in office. However, it will require vigilance and action so that the cabal agents of doom and gloom do not have their way.

If Mr. Trump's is not re-elected in 2020, it could result in an avalanche of socialist policies created by the democrats' progressive agenda, reversing all the good Trump has done and then unleashing all manner of evil on our country and the world. Even if you disagree with some of the President's styles and idiosyncrasies, we must unite behind his policies to reject the leftist rule that will bring us to the edge of destruction. I reiterate we must open our eyes to the pervasive occult influences corrupting not just in our federal government, Congress, the intelligence community, our media, and more broadly in our culture. These radical influences are evident across this country from the police-attacking thugs and destruction of private property across the country to the progressively ruled cities that have suffered from financial, moral, and social decline. The once beautiful streets of cities like Portland have degenerated into feces-infested streets, broken shop windows, drug-infested areas with gangs that have taken over parts of our country. Their protests turned into destructive riots where hatred and death have taken over.

It is the time to focus on the critical 2020 presidential election. In our hands, we hold the future of American. Be aware of what's at stake. We cannot sit in darkness and convince the night not to be dark. But we can eliminate the darkness by flooding it with light! That light must shine from the heavenly realms and be reflected in our homes, our churches and our hearts. Abraham Lincoln said, "The best way to predict your future is to create it."

It is our opportunity to unite regardless of party, race, or religion and stand united for our families and friends. The enemy is at the gate, but he will not prevail against us. It is not the time to be divided, nor the time to retreat or cover our faces. We must fight the good fight. We must continue to stand for truth and spread peace throughout the land. This is the day of the Lord, a day to recover what has been robbed from us. Reverse the curse and let freedom ring!

2

ANGEL OF LIBERTY

GEORGE WASHINGTON'S PROPHETIC
VISIONS

Throughout the American Revolution, there were moments when General George Washington would rather be at his Mount Vernon home. Despite his wishes, from the moment he accepted his appointment as the Commander in Chief of the Continental Army in 1775 until after the American victory at Yorktown in 1781, Washington never returned to his beloved home on the Potomac.

During the war for independence from England, Washington would survive multiple defeats at the hands of the British army, mutiny, lack of support from Congress, and, foremost, the brutal winter at Valley Forge with his beleaguered army.

Twelve thousand men with approximately five hundred women and children accompanied Washington on the march to Valley Forge, located twenty miles northwest of Philadelphia. Washington picked Valley Forge because it was close enough to keep an eye on the British sheltered in Philadelphia, yet far enough away to prevent a surprise attack on his own Continental Army. Washington and his men remained at the camp for approximately six months, from December 1777 until June 1778.

Washington's army survived legendary suffering in the march to victory. The images of bloody footprints in the snow, soldiers starving while huddled around lonely campfires, and Washington on his knees, praying that his army would survive to remind us of the great sacrifices made fighting for freedom. He hoped his officers and soldiers would surmount the troubles staring at them, with one heart and one mind.

"The freezing weather and starvation at Valley Forge were not even the most dangerous threats: diseases proved to be the biggest killer. As the National Park Service says, "Disease was the true scourge of the camp." By the end of the six-month encampment, some 2,000 men—roughly one in six—died of disease. Camp records indicate that two-thirds of the deaths happened during the warmer months of March, April and May when soldiers were less confined to their cabins and food and other supplies were more abundant."[1]

The six-month encampment at Valley Forge from 1777-1778 was a significant turning point in the American Revolutionary War. While conditions were notoriously cold and harsh and provisions were in short supply, it was at the winter camp where George Washington proved his leadership. With the help of former Prussian military officer, Friedrich Wilhelm Baron von Steuben, Washington transformed a battered Continental Army into a unified, world-class fighting force capable of beating the British.

ANGEL OF LIBERTY: GEORGE WASHINGTON'S PROPHETIC VISIONS

All the newspapers were writing about Washington and his rebel faction and how the British were mocking and laughing at him, saying "He has no chance." Sound familiar? Up until this point, Washington had lost many battles and suffered extensive losses. Despite the ridicule, Washington was often seen going into the thicket to pray and ask God for one more breath to push forward. It was at this moment that an angel visited Washington. The story was buried in the archives of American history until it was printed in the National Tribune.

In the National Tribune, 1880, an article appeared, giving an account of the "Vision of Washington" at Valley Forge. The National Tribune is now called The Stars and Stripes. This article was reprinted in the Stars and Stripes on December 21, 1950.

The account was told by a gentleman named Anthony Sherman, who was at Valley Forge during that brutal winter. The story has been published several times.

"The soldier mentioned as having a first-hand account of the "Vision," Anthony Sherman, was a soldier in the Continental Army. However, according to his pension application, written by him, he states that he was at Saratoga under the command of Benedict Arnold at the end of 1777 and only joined the main forces in 1778 in New Jersey just before the Battle of Monmouth.

"Anthony Sherman wrote: You doubtless heard the story of Washington's going to the thicket to pray in secret for aid and comfort from God, the interposition of whose Divine Providence

brought us safely through the darkest days of tribulation. One day, I remember it well, when the chilly winds whistled through the leafless trees, though the sky was cloudless and the sun shone brightly, he remained in his quarters nearly all the afternoon alone. When he came out, I noticed that his face was a shade paler than usual. There seemed to be something on his mind of more than ordinary importance." [2]

Returning just after dusk, Washington dispatched an orderly to the quarters who were presently in attendance. After a preliminary conversation of about an hour, and giving strict orders to not be disturbed, Washington, gazing upon his companion with that strange look of dignity which he alone commanded, related the event that day.

Washington shares his visions in first person narrative, without editing.

AN UNINVITED GUEST

This afternoon, as I was sitting at this table engaged in preparing a dispatch, something seemed to disturb me. Looking up, I beheld standing opposite me a singularly beautiful female. So astonished was I, for I had given strict orders not to be disturbed, that it was some moments before I found language to inquire the cause of her presence. A second, a third and even a fourth time did I repeat my question but received no answer from my mysterious visitor except a slight raising of her eyes.

By this time, I felt strange sensations spreading through me. I would have risen but the riveted gaze of the being before me rendered volition impossible. I assayed once more to address her, but my tongue had become useless, as though it had become paralyzed.

A new influence, mysterious, potent, irresistible, took possession of me. All I could do was to gaze steadily, vacantly at my unknown visitor. Gradually the surrounding atmosphere seemed as if it had become filled with sensations, and luminous.

Everything about me seemed to rarefy, the mysterious visitor herself becoming more airy and yet more distinct to my sight than before. I now began to feel as one dying, or rather to experience the sensations which I have sometimes imagined accompany dissolution. I did not think, I did not reason, I did not move; all were alike, impossible. I was only conscious of gazing fixedly, vacantly at my companion. [3]

THE FIRST GREAT PERIL - REVOLUTIONARY WAR

Presently I heard a voice saying, "*Son of the Republic, look and learn,*" while at the same time my visitor extended an arm eastwardly, I now beheld a heavy white vapor at some distance rising fold upon fold. This gradually dissipated, and I looked upon a stranger scene. Before me lay spread out in one vast plain all the countries of the world — Europe, Asia, Africa and America. I saw rolling and tossing between Europe and America the billows of the Atlantic, and between Asia and America lay the Pacific.

"Son of the Republic," said the same mysterious voice as before, *"look and learn."* At that moment I beheld a dark, shadowy being, like an angel, standing or rather floating in mid-air, between Europe and America. Dipping water out of the ocean in the hollow of each hand, he sprinkled some upon America with his right hand, while with his left hand he cast some on Europe. Immediately a cloud raised from these countries and joined in mid-ocean. For a while it remained stationary, and then moved slowly westward, until its enveloped America in its murky folds. Sharp flashes of lightning gleamed through it at intervals, and I heard the smothered groans and cries of the American people. [4]

SECOND GREAT PERIL - CIVIL WAR

A second time the angel dipped water from the ocean and sprinkled it out as before. The dark cloud was then drawn back to the ocean, in whose heaving billows sank from view. A third time I heard the mysterious voice saying, *"Son of the Republic, look and learn,"* I cast my eyes upon America and beheld villages and towns and cities springing up one after another until the whole land from the Atlantic to the Pacific was dotted with them.

Again, I heard the mysterious voice say, *"Son of the Republic, the end of the century cometh, look and learn."* At this the dark shadowy angel turned his face southward, and from Africa I saw an ill-omened specter approach our land. It flitted slowly over every town and city. The inhabitants presently set themselves in battle array against each other. As I continued looking I saw a bright angel, on whose brow rested a crown of light, on which was traced the word *"Union,"* bearing the American flag which he placed between the divided nation, and said, "Remember ye are brethren." Instantly, the inhabitants, casting from them their weapons became friends once more, and united around the National Standard.

THIRD GREAT PERIL - TODAY

PERSONAL NOTE BY AUTHOR: *Even today as I write the pages to this book, they are attempting to pull down our national monuments and memorial. They are burning our cities and looting our businesses. They want to defund the police and make cities sovereign nations in an attempt to change the course of the United States of America and undermine our heritage along with the sacrifice of untold hundreds of thousands, even millions who paid the ultimate price for our values and freedom.*

And again, I heard the mysterious voice saying, *"Son of the Republic, look and learn."* At this the dark, shadowy angel placed a trumpet to his mouth, and blew three distinct blasts; and taking water from the ocean, he sprinkled it upon Europe, Asia and Africa. Then my eyes beheld a fearful scene: From each of these countries arose thick, black clouds that were soon joined into one. Throughout this mass there gleamed a dark red light by which I saw hordes of armed men, who, moving with the cloud, marched by land and sailed by sea to America. Our country was enveloped in this volume of cloud, and I saw these vast armies devastate the whole county and burn the villages, towns and cities that I beheld springing up.

As my ears listened to the thundering of the cannon,

clashing of sword, and the shouts and cries of millions in mortal combat, I heard again the mysterious voice saying, *"Son of the Republic, look and learn."*

When the voice had ceased, the dark shadowy angel placed his trumpet once more to his mouth and blew a long and fearful blast. Instantly a light of a thousand suns shone down from above me and pierced and broke into fragments the dark cloud which enveloped America. At the same moment the angel upon whose head still shone the word Union, and who bore our national flag in one hand and a sword in the other, descended from the heavens attended by legions of white spirits. These immediately joined the inhabitants of America, who I perceived were exhausted and near overcome, but who immediately taking courage again, closed up their broken ranks and renewed the battle. Again, amid the fearful noise of the conflict, I heard the mysterious voice saying,

"Son of the Republic, look and learn." As the voice ceased, the shadowy angel for the last time dipped water from the ocean and sprinkled it upon America. Instantly the dark cloud rolled back, together with the armies it had brought, leaving the inhabitants of the land victorious!

Then once more I beheld the villages, towns and cities springing up where I had seen them before, while the bright angel, planting the azure standard he had brought in the midst of them, cried with a loud voice: "While the stars remain, and the heavens send down dew upon the earth, so long shall the Union last." And taking from his brow the crown on which blazoned the word *"Union,"* he placed it upon the Standard while the people, kneeling down, said, "Amen."

The scene instantly began to fade and dissolve, and I at last saw nothing but the rising, curling vapor I at first beheld. This also disappearing, I found myself once more gazing upon the mysterious visitor, who, in the same voice I had heard before, said,

"Son of the Republic," *what you have seen is thus interpreted: Three great perils will come upon the Republic. The most fearful is the third, but in this greatest conflict the whole world united shall not prevail against her.* *Let every child of the Republic learn to live for his God, his land and the Union."* [5]

THE INTERPRETATION

The scene instantly began to fade and dissolve, and I, at last saw nothing but the rising, curling vapor I at first beheld. This also disappeared, and I found myself once more gazing upon the mysterious visitor, who, in the same voice I had heard before, said, 'Son of the Republic, what you have seen is thus interpreted; Three great perils will come upon the Republic.

The most fearful for her is the third. But the whole world united shall not prevail against her. Let every child of the Republic learn to live for his God, his land, and UNION" With these words the vision vanished, and I started from my seat and felt that I had seen a vision wherein had been shown me **the birth, the progress, and the destiny of the United States."** [6]

THE EXPLANATION

While writing this chapter, I felt compelled to share George Washington's vision in its totality without editing. I wanted the reader to enjoy the completed picture that artistically detailed the nature and message of the angelic visitation. It's obvious that the first and second peril refers to the Revolutionary and Civil Wars to be fought inside the country. As the angel stated, the third peril was the most fearful and dangerous.

"Son of the Republic, what you have seen is thus interpreted: Three great perils will come upon the Republic. The most fearful is the third, but in this greatest conflict the whole world united shall not prevail against her. Let every child of the Republic learn to live for his God, his land and the Union."

This third and final peril appear as the dark clouds of invading forces seek to destroy the Republic. Though the angel uses war and battle vernacular, combined with descriptions of fighting conflict, it's clear that this enemy is not an invading army, but rather a dark demonic principality. It is a prophetic cloud aimed at destroying this nation through dark spiritual forces from both outside and within the nation. Look again at what the angel said.

"Son of the Republic, look and learn." When the voice had ceased, the dark shadowy angel placed his trumpet once more to his mouth and blew a long and fearful blast.

When the voice had ceased, the dark shadowy angel placed his trumpet once more to his mouth and blew a long and fearful blast. Instantly a light of a thousand suns shone down from above me and pierced and broke into fragments the dark cloud which enveloped America.

This third and great "Peril" that George Washington saw in the vision commenced with the dark shadowy angel placing his mouth, and at the sound of the TRUMP created a long fearful blast. This "dark shadowy angel" is distinct from the dark cloud with red eyes. This angel is a messenger of the Lord, an agent of God sent to conduct heaven's will. This Angel blew a long fearful blast on the TRUMP and, *"Instantly, a light of a thousand suns shone down from above me and pierced and broke into fragments the dark cloud which enveloped America."*

It is clear that when all seems lost in this Third Great Peril that heaven intervenes on behalf of an exhausted people while saving a great nation.

The first two Great Perils have come to pass. The stories are recorded in American history in painful, but triumphant detail. The third and most frightening *peril* is happening in our nation right now. However, I believe that God has sovereignly determined the final victory. Through the appointed angel, God showed the first President, who was the Commander and Chief and newly elected leader of this great nation. God cares for the **"Sons of the Republic"** and will guide and protect us. For those that might have forgotten, a republic is a state in which the supreme power rests in the body of citizens entitled to vote and is exercised by representatives chosen directly or indirectly by them.

THE TRUMP WILL SOUND WITH HELP FROM HEAVEN

The media mocked and ridiculed Trump and his "deplorable" followers. The daily narrative of the fake media was relentless and predictable. Daily, the band of prejudiced commentators gathered at their desks and reported the same boring narrative.

"He doesn't have a chance" and "The polls all indicate a blue landslide on election day." Listening to the chatterboxes, one would get the impression that the election was already over, and Hillary Clinton would move into the White House.

BUT GOD ... intervened and against all the odds, Donald J. Trump was elected the 45th President of the United States of America. Do you remember Washington's vision when the angel put the TRUMP to his mouth and blew a long fearful blast? That was the day.

"Son of the Republic, look and learn." When the voice had ceased, the dark shadowy angel placed his trumpet once more to his mouth and blew a long and fearful blast.

When the voice had ceased, the dark shadowy angel placed his trumpet once more to his mouth and blew a long and fearful blast. Instantly a light of a thousand suns shone down from above me and pierced and broke into fragments the dark cloud which enveloped America.

In the game of spades, the trump card is the winning card. When you lay down a trump card during the game, you win and you take the whole trick. With pleasure, you pick up every card on the table.

God takes the whole trick and picks up everything on the table with His winning hand, which is the TRUMP CARD.

There is doubt that President TRUMP will secure a second term and will continue in a long fearful blast of his presidential administration. When he is elected to his second term, the TRUMP's blast will dishearten the principalities of the dark cloud with the red eyes. Many will fall due to the exposure of corruption and lawless acts. In this great day of the Lord, angelic forces will be released from heaven like the light of a thousand suns burning and fragmenting the dark cloud that once enveloped America.

As I write this book, I am watching the news. Many are tragically tearing down national monuments, burning bibles and our flag in the streets, wrecking buildings and cars, and terrorizing innocent people, trying to reshape history and build a new world order. If this were to happen, we would undoubtedly stumble blindly into an unknown future. The spiritual dark cloud of intentional evil would love nothing less than to destroy this great nation and cause it to forfeit its freedoms for which so many paid the ultimate price for freedom. **But it will not happen!**

When it seems as if all hope is lost, *the "TRUMP will Sound" and Instantly the light of a thousand suns will shine down from above, and pierce and break into fragments the dark cloud that is now enveloping America.* The dark nefarious cabal will be exposed from Wall Street to Washington D.C. At the highest level, government corruption will be exposed to the world. Many will be brought to justice under the law, as Lady Liberty continues to proudly extend the torch of freedom in her right-hand demanding equality, liberty, and justice for all.

After the dark cloud had been rolled away, General George Washington saw America springing up again.

"Then once more I beheld the villages, towns and cities springing up where I had seen them before, while the bright angel, planting the azure standard he had brought in the midst of them, cried with a loud voice: "While the stars remain, and the heavens send down dew upon the earth, so long shall the Union last." And taking from his brow the crown on which blazoned the word "Union," he placed it upon the Standard while the people, kneeling down, said, "Amen."

The angel concludes with this glorious declaration.

"The most fearful is the Third Peril, but in this greatest conflict (which I believe we are in right now) the whole world united shall not prevail against her. Let every child of the Republic learn to live for his God, his land and the Union."

According to the vision, America's noblest days are ahead. We will not fall to evil forces or influences. Yes, there are still battles ahead of us like abortion, gay marriage, pedophilia, and sex trafficking. Nevertheless, by God's grace and help, we will prevail, and America will remain the greatest nation on the planet. Let the echo of the angel's words ring in your ears:

"Let every child of the Republic learn to live for his God, his land and the Union. And as the stars remain, and the heavens send down dew upon the earth, so long shall the Union last."

There is an 'if' attached to every victory. *If My people who are called by My name will humble themselves, and pray and seek My face, and turn from their wicked ways, then I will hear from heaven, and will forgive their sin and heal their land.*[7] National repentance and reformation is the demand and national mercy is the promise,

The reality of the divine presence is attested by the miracle, which is the miracle of forgiveness and healing of the nation. Empowered by God's presence, we will become activists for the kingdom, and under His direction, we will usher in a Kingdom order, as we tear down the feeble attempts of ungodly forces seeking to initiate their corrupted order. This was Washington's dream and the dream of the Republic.

> Blessed is the nation whose God is the LORD, the people whom He has chosen for His own inheritance. [8]

3

A FOUR HUNDRED YEAR DESTINY DOOR

Acongregation of approximately four hundred English Puritans living in exile in Leiden, Holland, was determined to purge the Church of England of what they felt were many excesses and abuses. But rather than work for change in England, they chose to live as separatists in religiously tolerant Holland in 1608. As separatists, they were considered illegal radicals by their home country of England. [1]

In explaining to his congregation why they should emigrate, Robinson used the analogy of the ancient Israelites leaving Babylon to escape bondage by returning to Jerusalem, where they would build their temple. "The Pilgrims and Puritans actually referred to themselves as God's New Israel," wrote Peter Marshall. It was therefore the *manifest destiny* of the Puritans to similarly build a "spiritual Jerusalem" in America.[2]

Their desire to travel to America was considered audacious and risky, as previous attempts to settle in North America had failed. Jamestown, founded in 1607, saw most of its settlers die within the first year. 440 of the 500 new arrivals died of starvation during the first six months of winter. The Puritan separatists also learned of the constant threat of attacks by Indigenous peoples. But despite all the arguments against traveling to this new land, their conviction that God wanted them to go held sway: "We verily believe and trust the Lord is with us," they wrote, "and that He will graciously prosper our endeavors according to the simplicity of our hearts therein." [3]

After deciding to leave Holland, they planned to cross the Atlantic using two purchased ships. A small ship, with the name *Speedwell*, would first carry them from Leiden to England. Then, the larger *Mayflower* would be used to transport most passengers and supplies the rest of the way.

In early September, western gales turned the North Atlantic into a dangerous place to sail. The *Mayflower*'s provisions were already quite low when departing Southampton, and they became lower still by delays of more than a month. The passengers had been on board the ship this entire time, feeling worn out and in no condition for a very taxing, lengthy Atlantic journey cooped up in the cramped spaces of a small ship.

When the *Mayflower* sailed from Plymouth alone on September 6, 1620, with what Bradford called "a prosperous wind", she carried 102 passengers plus a crew of 25 to 30 officers and men, bringing the total aboard to approximately 130. [4]

"At last, the over-full and hitherto baffled *Mayflower* was ready for the third trial. This final voyage would be successful. On September 26, 1620, the gallant little craft slipped out to sea. In proportion to her cubic feet of space, no heavier cargo had ever been shipped across the Atlantic. The entirety of a new church, a new commonwealth, a new nation, all of which were to bless the world, were confined within the limits of the *Mayflower's* hold. The course of empire was moving westward indeed."[5]

The Mayflower set sail from England in July 1620, but it had to turn back twice because Speedwell was leaking. After deciding to leave the leaky Speedwell behind, Mayflower finally got underway on September 6, 1620. In the 1600s, the ocean was full of dangers. Ships could be attacked and taken over by pirates. Many ships in the 1600s were damaged or shipwrecked by storms. Passengers sometimes fell overboard and drowned or got sick and died.

Although the Mayflower did not sink, a few of these things did happen! Fortunately, the Mayflower wasn't taken over by pirates. The ship sailed on a northern path across the Atlantic to avoid the pirates, but she *was* damaged by a bad storm halfway to America. The storm cracked one of the massive wooden beams supporting the frame of the ship. Fortunately, the passengers brought along a "great iron screw," which helped raise the beam back into place so the ship could continue. In another storm, a young passenger, John Howland, was swept off the deck of the ship and into the ocean! He was saved because he grabbed onto one of the ship's ropes and was pulled back onto the deck.[6]

ARRIVAL IN CAPE COD, NOVEMBER 11, 1620

After roughly two miserable months at sea, the ship finally reached the New World. A few weeks later, they left Cape Cod and sailed up the coast to Plymouth and started to build their town where a group of Wampanoag People had lived before (a sickness had killed most of them). The Pilgrims lived on the ship for a few more months, rowing ashore to build houses during the day, and returning to the ship at night. Many people began to get sick from the cold and the wet; after all, it was December! About half the people on *Mayflower* died that first winter from what they described as a "general sickness" of colds, coughs, and fevers.

Finally, in March 1621, there were enough houses that everyone could live on land. After a long, hard voyage, and an even harder winter, *Mayflower* left Plymouth to return to England on April 5, 1621.[7]

MAYFLOWER COMPACT

The 1620 agreement, first called the *Mayflower Compact* in 1793, was a legal instrument that bound the Pilgrims together when they arrived in New England. The core members of the Pilgrims' immigrant group were Separatists, members of a Puritan sect that had split from the Church of England, the only legal church in England at that time. However, others in the group remained part of the Church of England. Not all of the Pilgrims shared the same religion.

When the Pilgrims left England, they obtained permission from the King of England to settle on land farther to the south near the mouth of the Hudson River in present-day New York. Because they chose to remain where they landed in New England, they needed a new permission (called a patent) to settle there. On November 11, 1620, needing to maintain order and establish a civil society while they waited for this new patent, the adult male passengers signed the *Mayflower Compact*.[8]

In 1802, John Quincy Adams described the agreement as "the only instance in human history of that positive, original, social compact" and it is popularly believed to have influenced the Declaration of Independence and the U.S. Constitution.

THE TEXT OF THE MAYFLOWER COMPACT:

In the name of God, We whose names are underwritten, the loyal subjects of our dread Sovereign Lord King James, by the Grace of God of Great Britain, France, and Ireland King, Defender of the Faith, etc.

Having undertaken for the Glory of God and advancement of the Christian Faith and Honour of our King and Country, a Voyage to plant the First Colony in the Northern Parts of Virginia, do by these presents solemnly and mutually in the presence of God and one of another, Covenant and Combine ourselves together in a Civil Body Politic, for our better ordering and preservation and furtherance of the ends aforesaid; and by virtue hereof to enact, constitute and frame such just and equal Laws, Ordinances, Acts, Constitutions and Offices from time to time, as shall be thought most meet and convenient for the general good of the Colony, unto which we promise all due submission and obedience.

In witness whereof we have hereunder subscribed our names at Cape Cod, the 11th of November, in the year of the reign of our Sovereign Lord King James, of England, France and Ireland the eighteenth, and of Scotland the fifty-fourth. Anno Domini 1620.[9]

A 400 YEAR DESTINY DOOR, 1620 TO 2020

At the beginning of 2020, I asked the Lord for insight and help understanding these testing times. I was reminded of **1 Chronicles 12:32**, *"of the sons of Issachar who had understanding of the times, to know what Israel ought to do, their chiefs were two hundred; and all their brethren were at their command."* The meteorologist *might be able to forecast the weather, but is the church able to understand the times?*

Through the night and morning hours, I spent long hours studying and reading and "listening prayer." While praying for the President and the coming elections, the Lord brought to my attention what I now call a "window of opportunity" or a "destiny door." We must synchronize our time with heaven's time to be positioned properly for windows of opportunity and doors of destiny. Prophetic timing is like a door lock. The tumblers in the lock need to be in alignment or the door will not open. All the conditions and circumstances must be arranged in perfect order for a reformation to happen. I do believe we are in a destiny door window of time.

In my prayerful study, one morning, the Lord showed me that what happened with the 1620 Mayflower landing at Cape Cod was key to the events that are happening now in our nation.

The Mayflower set anchor in the bay of Cape Cod, Plymouth Rock, November 11, 1620. From 11/11/1620 till 11/11/2020 marks the 400th anniversary of this event. Immediately, I saw the connection. I envisioned a link between America's founding and the Hebrews' exodus from Egypt. Israel and America arrived at the end of a 400- year cycle, leading to a door of destiny.

THE EXODUS FROM EGYPT

In the Jewish narrative, Joseph was sold into slavery by his jealous brothers and rose to become *vizier*, the second most powerful man in Egypt next to Pharaoh. His presence and office saved Israel in a time of crisis. Towards the end of the Bronze Age, in the last decades of the 13th century and the early decades of the 12th century B.C.E., the Mediterranean world suffered a decades-long series of draughts and famines.

Because of the divine favor on his life and the supernatural ability to interpret dreams, he was elevated from a dungeon to Egypt's highest political positions. With almost absolute economic control of Egypt, Joseph led them through a severe crisis. By his leadership, Joseph also saved his father, Jacob, and his brothers. For a season during and after Joseph's death, Israelites prospered in number and resources in Egypt. But things changed.

"There arose a new king over Egypt, who did not know Joseph." (Exodus 1:8)

This lack of knowledge reflected the lapse of national memory concerning the historic role Joseph and the Israelites previously played in the nation's success.

Instead of policies based on commemorative appreciation, fear was the power shaping new policies. Over time, the brutalizing patterns of fear led to the loss of dignity and protection, then to shame, then to public outcry against them, and finally to the enslavement of the Israelites. Sound familiar? Now, it is happening in America.

The Israelites were afflicted in Egypt for four hundred years.

God said to Abram, "Know for sure that your descendants will be strangers [living temporarily] in a land (Egypt) that is not theirs, where they will be enslaved and oppressed for four hundred years. But on that nation whom your descendants will serve I will bring judgment, and afterward they will come out [of that land] with great possessions. (Genesis 15:13-14)

MYSTERY OF VIRGINIA'S FIRST SLAVES

The four-hundred-year mark establishes the boundaries of Israel's growth and influence in Egypt. It also frames a tragic picture of how Joseph was forgotten, and the Hebrews became slaves.

There is another 400-year event of historical and yet grim significance, similar to the Hebrew enslavement. A 2006 article in the Washington Post, entitled *Mystery of Virginia's First Slaves Is Unlocked 400 Years Later,*" provides the historical background of the twenty or so Africans who arrived in Jamestown. For nearly 400 years, historians believed they were transported to Virginia from the West Indies on a Dutch warship. Little else was known of the Africans, who left no trace.

New scholarship coupled with transatlantic detective work solved the puzzle of who they were and where their forced journey across the Atlantic Ocean began.[10]

The name "Angela" reflects a woman from Angola who was identified by that English name in the 1624 census and who arrived in 1619. The landing of these first Africans in the English colony began a process that ultimately led to full slavery of millions of Africans in the colonies. The racial divide in the United States has deep and wide root.

On January 1, 1863, President Lincoln formally issued the Emancipation Proclamation, calling on the Union army to liberate all slaves as "an act of justice, warranted by the Constitution, upon military necessity." These three million slaves were declared to be "then, thenceforward, and forever free. As the confederacy staggered toward defeat, Lincoln realized that the Emancipation Proclamation, a war measure, might have little constitutional authority once the war was over. The Republican Party subsequently introduced the 13th Amendment into Congress, and in April 1864 the necessary two-third of the overwhelmingly Republican senate passed the amendment. However, the House of Representatives, featuring a higher proportion of Democrats, did not pass the amendment until January 1865.[11]

It is a sad tale of the interconnection between greed, political power, sexual abuse, and the dehumanizing of millions of people. When the Lord spoke to Abraham in Genesis 15 concerning his descendant's four-hundred-year oppression in Egypt, the Lord promised that He would "judge" Egypt and that the Israelites would come out of that oppression "with great possessions" (Genesis 15:14).

The word "judge" signifies that the Lord contends for and vindicates Israel in their struggle against Egypt. I cannot help but think of the American Civil War from 1861 to1865 as an act of divine judgment upon our entire nation. These lyrics in *The Battle Hymn of the Republic* highlight God's judgment. He <God> is trampling out the vintage where the grapes of wrath are stored, He hath loosed the fateful lightning of His terrible swift sword."

Then in 1964, the Civil Rights Act ended segregation in public places and banned employment discrimination based on race, color, religion, sex, or national origin. It is considered one of the crowning legislative achievements of the civil rights movement. First proposed by President John F. Kennedy, it survived strong opposition from southern Democrat members of Congress and was signed into law by Kennedy's successor, Lyndon B. Johnson. In subsequent years, Congress expanded the act and passed additional civil rights legislation such as the Voting Rights Act of 1965.[12]

There were two friends, two prophets standing together during the civil rights movement. One was Martin Luther King Jr., and the other was Rabbi Abraham Heschel. Were Heschel and King the prophets of America? Neither claimed the title, but each spoke of the other as a prophet. In introducing King to the audience, Heschel asked, "Where in American today do we hear a voice like the voice of the prophets of Israel? Martin Luther King is a sign that God has not forsaken the United States of America. God has sent him to us. His presence is the hope of America. His mission is sacred, his leadership of supreme importance, to every one of us."

In response, King stated that Heschel "is indeed a truly great prophet...Here and there we find those who refuse to remain silent behind the security of stained-glass windows, and they are forever seeking to make the great ethical insights of our Judeo-Christian heritage relevant in this day and in this age." [13]

LEARNING TO TRUST A GOD OF MIRACLES

Here we are, four hundred years and counting. We know how the Exodus story concluded. The Hebrew slaves of Egypt were delivered by the power of signs, wonders, and miracles. It was nothing short of God's miraculous hand that delivered them from the bonds of slavery, from which they were unable to free themselves. God's supernatural hand delivered them through the Red Sea, busting the 400-year old oppressors, and supernaturally guided and provided for them through the wilderness as they journeyed to the Promised Land.

After the meeting with Melchizedek, Abraham had a dream.

"Now when the sun was going down, a deep sleep fell upon Abram; and behold, horror and great darkness fell upon him. Then He said to Abram: "Know certainly that your descendants will be strangers in a land that is not theirs, and will serve them, and they will afflict them **four hundred years.**"[14]

Since Abraham's dream, the Jewish memories had faded. They had endured the hardship of slavery under the Egyptians. All that remained was the Jewish records of their history. The Hebrews had been assimilated into the Egyptian culture.

As the generations passed, the Israelites barely remembered the God of their forefathers, nor did they recollect God's manifest miracles. After 400 years of heaven's silence, God anointed Moses to be His deliverer. At the burning bush we are reminded of the historic words spoken by God. "*Then the LORD said unto*

Moses, Go in unto Pharaoh, and tell him, Thus says the LORD God of the Hebrews, Let my people go, that they may serve me." [15]

Let my people go became Moses announcement in the face of Pharaoh. In the middle of the night, after 210 years of slavery, 600,000 men between the ages of 18 and 60, left Egypt. Almost three million people marched for three days. However, by the time the Hebrews reached the Red Sea, Pharaoh's heart was hardened, and the entire Egyptian army was in full pursuit.

There was nowhere for the Hebrew slaves to go. They could either surrender and go back to Egypt or forge ahead into the sea. The former slaves were frightened and screamed to turn back, not wanting to die in the wilderness.

But Moses and Aaron stood firm. Creating a strong east wind against the sea, God caused the waters to part so the Jews could march through. With their heavy metal armor and heavy chariots and horses, the Egyptians pursued them. When the last Jew had crossed the sea, God caused the waters to fall back, drowning the Egyptian army. Only Pharaoh was spared. He stood transfixed on the shore. He had no choice but to watch in horror as his entire army vanished beneath the waves.

There was great rejoicing from the other side. Miriam, Moses's older sister, gathered the women and began singing and dancing in praise of God. Now that they were free, God required Israel to put their trust in Him. Their GPS was a supernatural cloud by day and pillar of fire by night. They had to trust their lives and destiny to an unseen force of which they were unfamiliar. God revealed Himself to Israel demonstrating He could deliver them through supernatural demonstrations of signs wonders and miracles. During the day, God provided heavenly mana to feed the masses of people and animals. Water gushed from a Rock that seemed to follow them, and we know that the Rock was Christ.

> For I do not want you to be unaware, believers, that our fathers were all under the cloud [in which God's presence went before them] and they all passed [miraculously and safely] through the [Red] Sea; And all [of them] were baptized into Moses [into his safekeeping as their leader] in the cloud and in the sea; and all [of them] ate the same spiritual food; and all [of them] drank the same spiritual drink, for they were drinking from a spiritual rock which followed them; and the Rock was Christ. 16

Like Israel, God set America free. God's supernatural hand is evident throughout our history and to maintain that freedom require trust in God and resisting any attempt to rob us of the divine gift. American is more than just a place; it is an ideal and a set of principles. In America, the government exists for and with the consent of the people.

It was a radical concept in the beginning that the founders knew would require informed and responsible citizens who remain vigilant. Enjoying the privilege of a free society, it is compulsory each American pray and play their part preserving the nation's ideals of freedom.

Freedom is an inherently spiritual attribute underlying the evolutionary process of freedom. This should always be remembered as a compelling and commanding reality by all people everywhere. We have survived eons of opposition from the principle of enslaving selfishness and is mainly responsible, at this time, for the struggle in which we are all participating. The miraculous events culminating in creating the United States of America in the 1700s changed the world. No other society before then and since has come close to to the impact America has had on the world. The technological advances led by American ideas and innovation has spread throughout the world to the benefit of billions of people.

We must continue to stand fast during these days as we guard our nation against any encroachment against the values we hold dear.

4

THE THIRD GREAT AWAKENING

I believe that numbers and dates have prophetic significance. Chapter three tracks the Mayflower's path from when it dropped the anchor in the bay of Cape Cod on November 11,1620. Calculating the numerical sequence between11-11-1620 and 11-11-2020, we arrive at 400 years. This year we celebrate the 400th anniversary that I believe points prophetically to a nation on the verge of another Great Awakening, both governmentally and spiritually. Remember that God counted the days of creation. The stars are numbered, the grains of sand in the sea are numbered, Jesus said even the very hairs of your head are numbered. Biblical numbers are used in prophecy of time and cycles. *He determines the number of the stars and calls them each by name* (Psalm 147:4).

The interpretation of numbers in the Bible is quite different from how numbers are interpreted under popular numerological methods. "The Jewish numerology tradition, known as gematria, values some numbers more than others. The practice of gematria, or the spiritual interpretation of numbers, is one technique for understanding sacred texts. Some numbers are considered symbolic and or sacred in Judaism."[1]

> How precious also are Your thoughts to me, Oh God, How vast is the sum of them. If I could count them, they would outnumber the sand (Psalm 139:17-18).

> Are not five sparrows sold for two copper coins? Yet not one of them has [ever] been forgotten in the presence of God. Indeed, the very hairs of your head are all numbered. Do not be afraid; you are far more valuable than many sparrows (Luke 12:6-7).

I am not trying to overemphasize the significance of numbers, but some numbers have prophetic implications that cannot be ignored.

> After saying these things, he said to them, "Our friend Lazarus has fallen asleep, but I must go to **awaken** him" (John 11:11).

> *By faith Sarah herself received "power" to conceive, even when she was past the age, since she considered Him faithful who had promised* (Hebrews 11:11).

NUMERICAL INTERPRETATION AND INSIGHT

Interestingly enough, the Presidential Elections will be held November 3rd, and eight days later, on 11/11, we celebrate the 400 years after the landing of the Mayflower at Plymouth Rock.

The number "Eight" is always the number of new beginnings

as "Seven" refers to completion. As a prophet, I see the numerical sequence and meaning, as historical dates unfold, and events become stamped with the prophetic revelation concerning the current events of America's destiny.

In his farewell speech, President George Washington spoke these words. *"The name American, which belongs to you, in your national capacity, must always exalt the just pride of patriotism more than any appellation (name or title) derived from local discriminations."*

There have been two Great Awakenings in American history, the *"First Great Awakening"* from the 1730s to the 1740s, and the *"Second Great Awakening"* from 1785 to 1835. I envision a *"Third Great Awakening"* that will crash upon the shores of America that will reawaken and revive the nation spiritually, governmentally, and patriotically.

THE PEOPLES' PARTY

From the beginning of this nation, we have had two major parties, Republicans and Democrats. There have always been independent parties flirting with the elections in the background, In the not too distant future, I see a newly reformed party coming on the scene. It will be the *"Party of the People"* or the *"People's Party."* In essence, it will be an independent third party, with the backing of the people's reform of the *"New America,"* This third party will not replace Democratic or Republican parties, still it will represent the newly inspired patriotic citizens of the United States of America. The real America will fully embrace this new party due to the betrayal and disappointment of the political pollution that has overtaken both Democrats and

Republicans and will serve as a cleansing platform for the future of American politics. This third party will be the dominant party and become the norm as people are once again refreshed and renewed in the confidence of our constitutional premise that the Union is a *"Government of the people, by the people, for the people, that shall not perish from the earth."* (Abraham Lincoln Gettysburg Address)

As the Mayflower anchored on 11-11-1620, a John 11:11 Lazarus Awakening is happening in this nation that will embolden the people to rise into new strength and power for God and country. Patriotism, the love of God and country, will cause the Union to not stand anymore for radical left-wing ideology. This life and liberty of God and country will lead to the dispersing and exposing of the deep state nefarious underground activity, including trafficking and the unthinkable evil and corruption.

Many will be exposed as traitors of the Union, when their hidden schemes of darkness come to light. As it happened with General George Washington at Valley Forge, this Four Hundred year Destiny Door, 11-11-1620 to 11-11-2020, will give way to another divine intervention as the *"GOD OF AMERICA"* overthrows cowardly corrupt systems and people who have given themselves over to the lesser gods of the cabal and secret societies. These dark occult practitioners have secretly stolen and deceived the pure and guiltless by their dark intentional evil acts that include legalized abortion, abduction and murder of innocent children, and adults, trafficking, and the more than 800,000 innocent children that go missing every year. These satanic practitioners of evil will be exposed from Wall Street to Washington and everything in between while watching the *"GOD OF*

AMERICA" fighting for the innocence of a nation whose freedom and future are at stake.

The devil always overplays his hand. Those responsible may laugh and mock now, but they will be put to shame. Just as heaven intervened and fought for Israel's exodus from Egypt, heaven will again defend America as God intervenes supernaturally. It is a time of cleansing in America. The dark clouds George Washington witnessed in his epic angelic visitation will be displaced and dispersed by the blast of the TRUMP.

Just when it seems as if all hope is lost, *the "TRUMP will Sound" and instantly the light of a thousand suns will shine down from above, and pierce and break into fragments the dark cloud that is now enveloping America.*

I declare that a new era and time of healing of this nation is coming when help comes from heaven, similar to when God delivered the Hebrew people in Egypt. The light of a thousand suns of angels assist us in pushing back the darkness and establishing the banner of our true American destiny and flag and ideals to a renewed America.

Remember that after the dark cloud was rolled away, General George Washington saw America springing up again.

"Then once more I beheld the villages, towns and cities springing up where I had seen them before, while the bright angel, planting the azure standard he had brought in the midst of them, cried with a loud voice: "While the stars remain, and the heavens send down dew upon the earth, so long shall the Union last." And taking from his brow the crown on which blazoned the word "Union," he placed it upon the Standard while the people, kneeling down, said, "Amen."

According to the vision of the Lord, America's greatest days are ahead. We will not fall to evil forces or influences. Yes, some things need to be addressed and cleaned up such as abortion and gay marriage, but America is still the greatest nation on the planet.

THE ANGEL BREAKTHROUGH AND REVIVAL IN AMERICA

Years ago, Bob Jones had an encounter with an angel whose name was "Breakthrough." He was assigned to the United States for three coming great revivals. Bob later stated that this was one of the most profound and significant visitations he had ever received.

On Friday, March 24th, 2004, as Bob was waiting on the Lord in prayer, he went into an Acts 10:10 type of trance. As the visitation commenced, Bob saw what appeared to be twelve ordinary "men" approaching him. Although they had the appearance of men, he knew they were angels. The one in front seemed to be the most prominent and he served as spokesman for the group.

The angel said, *"My name is 'Breakthrough, and I have now been assigned to the United States for the coming great revivals."* For approximately 30 minutes, the angel shared with Bob historical accounts of past revivals that transpired in which he was involved. The angel's task was to release breakthrough and awakening initiating a wave of harvest by first extracting all obstacles to God's plans, while other angels gather the harvest.

Most prominently, the angel shared his influence on the life of Benson Idahosa. Without Bob knowing Idahosa's history, the angel shared with Bob the great revivals that brought many souls into God's Kingdom in Nigeria. The angel explicitly stated that he has been in the United States the past two years, laying the groundwork for the next revival that stadiums would not be adequate to hold.

The angel "Breakthrough" continued speaking to Bob about God's end-time strategy. There were "11" other angels with him that were "Resurrection angels," and he explained how resurrections would become common in the coming revival. He shared how Benson Idahosa was commissioned to a nation, and no matter what the opposition was, the angel "Breakthrough" would remove all obstacles so that a harvest of souls could come. The angel then told Bob that everything he was observing in this vision was a prophecy of things to come.

At this point, he asked Bob this question. *"What do you see."* Bob replied, "Their appearance seemed so ordinary." The angel's response was "Precisely." He continued with these words. "We will work with ordinary people who have fully yielded spirit, soul, and body to the Lord."

MOVE, MOVE, MOVE: 3 MAJOR REVIVALS

Breakthrough then shouted, *"Move, Move, Move!"* By this, Bob knew that there would be at least three more major revivals to take place before the second coming of Jesus. It was also a clear directive for the church to move in faith. The angel said, *"We will be moving now with those that Move, Move, Move."* The angel quoted Matthew10 and then said, *"This is an end-time strategy that is to be employed now."*

And as you go, preach, saying, The kingdom of heaven is at hand.' Heal the sick, raise the dead, cleanse the lepers, cast out demons. Freely you received, freely give (Matthew 10:7-8).

It will be a season of harvest, a harvest of souls, and a harvest of promises. Even so, it will come not by the mere articulation of words, but also with power. That is the pattern of the early Church and the one we see demonstrated in the life and ministry of Benson Idahosa. Paul said he came not with words, but with a demonstration of power, and these coming revivals will be all of that and more.

And my message and my preaching were not in persuasive words of wisdom [using clever rhetoric], but [they were delivered] in demonstration of the [Holy] Spirit [operating through me] and of [His] power [stirring the minds of the listeners and persuading them] (1 Corinthians 2:4, AMP)

In Exodus 23, God promised to send an Angel before Israel to overcome every enemy and establish them in the land of promise. Their obedience to the Word assured them the victory and released the Lord to remove sickness from their midst. In like fashion, a wave of healing will accompany this season of grace we are now entering.

Behold, I send an Angel before you to keep you in the way and to bring you into the place which I have prepared. But if you truly obey his voice and do all that I say, then I will be an enemy to your enemies and an adversary to your adversaries. But you shall serve the Lord your God, and He will bless your bread and your water; and I will remove sickness from your midst. (Exodus 23:20, 22, 25)

In these last of revivals, the *"GOD OF AMERICA"* will overthrow the wicked and raise the standard of righteousness and justice throughout the land, providing peace and safety for a nation whose freedom and future are at stake. Get ready for the government to be shaken and for the nation to experience a spiritual awakening.

5

THE TRUE HISTORY OF PRESIDENT
DONALD J. TRUMP

The village of Tong, on the Outer Hebridean Island of Lewis, has a calm, unhurried disposition. The air is thick with the smell of fresh seaweed. The few dozen houses there are silhouetted against fields of peat colored in soft yellows, browns, and greens. In the near distance is Lewis' only town and the main source of jobs on the island.

The Scottish mainland is 40 miles, and a two-hour ferry-ride, away. With a population barely in three digits, Tong (pronounced "tongue") might seem a world away from the glassy opulence of Trump Tower or the gold-leafed walls of Mar-a-Lago to this flat, marshy land that Donald Trump traces his roots. His mother, Mary Anne MacLeod, was raised in the village, along with generations before her. She spoke almost exclusively in Scots Gaelic before leaving for a new life in the United States at age eighteen.

"Donald Trump owes much to his family, the MacLeod's of Scotland. Local records suggest his ancestors might be the source of Trump's first name and the original reddish tint of his hair. Trump attributes his flamboyance and appeal for entertainment to his Scottish side." [1]

"Looking back, I realize now that I got some of my sense of showmanship from my mother," he writes in his memoir *The Art of the Deal. "She always had a flair for the dramatic and the grand. She was a very traditional housewife, but she also had a sense of the world beyond her."*[2]

THE MACLEOD LEGACY

"Trump's great-great grandfather (and Alexander's father), Alasdair MacLeod, a fisherman born around 1810, was known by everyone as "Ruadh," or "Red," on account of his hair, perhaps the source of Trump's own infamous mop (which was more reddish-brown than cornmeal yellow in his younger days). He explained that Lewis was part of Norway until the 13th century. "Red hair is very common on the islands," Lawson said. "Almost everyone in the island, you trace back their DNA [and] you come to a Viking."[3]

The Tong that "Ruadh" knew, which subsisted mainly on fishing, farming and some weaving, was not an exceptionally hospitable place. "Ruadh" lost his life at sea around 1847. Donald Smith, Trump's great grandfather on his maternal grandmother's side, and perhaps his namesake met the same fate.

After Smith's death, his widow, Mary Smith, was left to manage the family croft, a small farm holding, and bring up their children. The youngest in the family, also named Mary, was Trump's grandmother. Her eventual husband, Malcolm

MacLeod, may be the source of some of Trump's entrepreneurial drive.

Born to Malcolm and Mary, on May 10, 1912, Mary Anne almost certainly would have lived in a narrow "black house"—so-called because of the soot that coated the thick stone walls, with a low, thatched roof. Tong's black houses are all gone today, replaced by large piles built on oil money from the North Sea (or, in the case of the MacLeod family plot, it was a more modern home). But a century ago they were still the most common family structure. Each member of the household would have been expected to help run the house and work the land.

"Raised in a Scottish Gaelic-speaking household, Mary was the youngest of ten children born to Malcolm (1866–1954) and Mary MacLeod (Smith; 1867–1963). Her father was a crofter, fisherman, and compulsory officer at Mary's school. English was her second language, which she learned at the school she attended until secondary school." [4]

"Her paternal grandparents were Alexander MacLeod and Ann MacLeod; her maternal grandparents were Donald Smith and Mary MacAulay. They were from the locations of Vatisker and South Lochs, and some of the family's generations had suffered in the Highland Clearances." [5]

Like most everyone else in Tong, the MacLeod's belonged to Scotland's Free Church, a Calvinist congregation with roots in the Scottish Reformation. The local church had a major bearing on everyday life in the village.

"In 1930, Mary Anne and her sister, Catherine, emigrated to America, hoping to find work. She found work as a nanny with a wealthy family in a big house in the suburbs of New York but lost the job as the US sank into depression after the Wall Street Crash. Mary Anne returned briefly to Scotland in 1934."[6]

'Six years later, she married successful property developer Frederick Trump, the son of German migrants and one of the most eligible men in New York. They fell in love. After they married in January 1936, they quickly began their family: Mary Ann Trump Barry, a United States Federal Judge (born 1937), Frederick Jr. (1938-1981), Elizabeth (born 1942), Donald, (1946), and Robert (1948). The fourth of their five children, Donald John, as he is referred to on the islands would become the 45th president of the United States. The couple lived in an affluent area of Queens and Mary Anne was active with charity work, when she met Frederick." [7]

THE HEBRIDES REVIVAL

"Two elderly sisters who desperately prayed to see God move in their small Scottish fishing village helped spark the movement between 1949 and 1952, known as the Hebrides Revival. In the late 1940s, Peggy and Christine Smith lived in a small cottage in Scotland on the Island of Lewis in the village of Barvas.

They were eighty-four and eighty-two years old. Peggy was blind, and her sister almost bent double with arthritis. Unable to attend public worship, their humble cottage became a sanctuary where they met with God. To them came the promise: "I will pour water upon him that is thirsty and floods upon the dry ground," they pleaded this day and night in prayer.

One night, Peggy had a revelation that revival was coming, and her father's church would be crowded again with young people! She sent for the minister, the Reverend James Murray

MacKay, and told him what God had shown her, asking him to call his elders and deacons together for special times of waiting upon God. In the same district, a group of men praying in a barn experienced a foretaste of coming blessing. One night as they waited upon God a young deacon rose and read part of the twenty-fourth Psalm:" [8]

> "Who shall ascend into the hill of the Lord? Or who shall stand in His holy place? He that hath clean hands and a pure heart; who hath not lifted up his soul unto vanity, nor sworn deceitfully. He shall receive the blessing from the Lord." (Psalm 24:3,4)

"Turning to the others, he said "Brethren, it seems to me just so much humbug to be waiting and praying as we are, if we are not rightly related to God." Then lifting his hands toward heaven, he cried: "Oh God, are my hands clean? Is my heart pure?" He got no further but fell prostrate to the floor. An awareness of God filled the barn and a stream of supernatural power was let loose in their lives. They had moved into a new sphere of God-realization, believing implicitly in the promise of revival."[9]

"Among those converted the following night was a fifteen-year-old boy who became an outstanding helper in the revival. This lad became a "frontline" prayer-warrior. The preacher, Duncan Campbell, called at his home one day and found him on his knees in the barn with the Bible open before him. When interrupted, he quietly said: *Excuse me a little, Mr. Campbell, I'm having an audience with the King.*" Some of the most vivid outpourings of the Spirit during the revival came when he was asked to pray. In the police station in Bravas, he stood up one night, simply clasped his hands together, and uttered one word – "Father." Everyone melted to tears as the Presence of God invaded the house. In Callenish, he prayed until the power of God laid hold on those who were dead in sins transforming them into living stones in the Church of Jesus Christ. But the most outstanding example of God's anointing upon him was in Bernera, a small island off the coast of Lewis."[10]

"Duncan was assisting at a Communion service; the atmosphere was heavy and preaching challenging, so he sent to Barvas for men to come and assist in prayer. They prayed, but the spiritual bondage persisted, so much so that halfway through his address Duncan stopped preaching. Just then, he noticed this boy visibly moved, under deep burden for souls. He thought: *"That boy is in touch with God and living nearer to the Savior than I am."* So, leaning over the pulpit, he said: "Donald, will you lead us in prayer?" The lad rose to his feet and in his prayer referred to the fourth chapter of Revelation, which he had been reading that morning:" [11]

"Oh God, I seem to be gazing through the open door. I see the Lamb in the midst of the Throne, with the keys of death and of hell at His girdle."

He began to sob; then lifting his eyes toward heaven, cried:

"O God, there is power there, let it loose!"

With the force of a hurricane the Spirit of God swept into the building and the floodgates of heaven opened. The church resembled a battlefield. Many were prostrated over the seats weeping and sighing; on the other hand, some were affected by throwing their arms in the air in a rigid posture. God had come!

Between 1949 and 1952 a wide-spread revival swept through these islands in answer to the prayers of God's people. This revival became known as the Hebrides Revival.

"Mary Anne Smith MacLeod, niece of the two intercessors of the Hebrides Revival, cousin of Donald Smith the 15 year old converted at the revival emigrated from the Hebridean Island of Lewis, off the west coast of Scotland, from where she emigrated to America and met a gentleman named Frederick Trump."[12]

THE REVIVAL BIBLE

Could a Bible sitting in the Oval Office be America's connection to a coming revival? Yes, President Donald Trump's roots reach back to one of the greatest revivals in history. What many don't know is that Trump's Bible has historic significance of its own.

"The one elderly sister who had prayed for revival sent her Bible to America as a gift to Mary Anne, the same Bible the elderly sister used in the Hebrides Revival of 1949 to 1952. President Donald Trump's Bible was a gift from his Bible-believing mother. Today, this Bible lies in her son's office, the Oval Office, at the White House and it was one of the Bibles upon which he placed his hand to take the oath of office. Could this point towards the re-digging of past wells of revival for the future?"[13]

God used two elderly sisters who desperately wanted to see God move in their church in a small fishing village on Lewis

Island. Not only did the revival reach their Island in Scotland but the Hebrides Revival became known around the world. Little did they know that their nephew would one day become the 45th President of the United States of America and bring change and a move of God to the Nations. It is time to rise up and intercede for our President and for our Nation.

"If my people, which are called by my name, shall humble themselves, and pray, and seek my face, and turn from their wicked ways; then will I hear from heaven, and will forgive their sin, and will heal their land" (2 Chronicles 7:14)

Pray for an awakening to invade the Oval Office and spread to every corner of the land. Never more than today has America needed the voices of the righteous. **This whole nation must be moved to prayer.** So great are the needs, so grave is the challenge, so colossal the problems that it is imperative we ascend before God's throne and lay hold of Him in prayer for our nation!

BILLY GRAHAM'S PRAYER FOR THE NATION

"Our Father and Our God, we praise You for Your goodness to our nation, giving us blessings far beyond what we deserve. Yet we know all is not right with America. We deeply need a moral and spiritual renewal to help us meet the many problems we face. Convict us of sin. Help us to turn to You in repentance and faith. Set our feet on the path of Your righteousness and peace. We pray today for our nation's leaders. Give them the wisdom to know what is right, and the courage to do it. You have said, 'Blessed is the nation whose God is the Lord.' May this be a new era for America, as we humble ourselves and acknowledge You alone as our Savior and Lord. This we pray in Your holy name, Amen."[14]

6

CIVIL WAR IN AMERICA

In early June of 2020, amid the Covid-19 Pandemic, I had a dream about a coming Civil War that shed immense light on the current status of the church. This dream is a prophetic picture and invitation for the church to be reawakened to the Holy Spirit's power, person, and presence

SID ROTH AND THE AMERICAN FLAG

In the early morning of June 12, 2020, I had a dream where I saw Sid Roth standing in our *Decoding the Supernatural* studio, created at the *"It's Supernatural Network"* complex in Charlotte. In the dream, Sid was standing in the studio with the American flag draped around his shoulders, and the stars on the flag were covering his right side. In the background, there was a Jewish flag gently swaying from a flagpole behind him. Suddenly, I saw what appeared to be a Civil War sword slicing down the middle of the screen and dividing the vision in two. At that moment, I heard the Lord speak.

"A Civil War is coming into the church that will divide it, and it is all around the person, power and Presence of the Holy Spirit."

In retrospect, I remember feeling a sense of excitement and dread while intensely observing the scene. I knew that we were entering a point of no return. In the dream, Sid Roth represented global media and gospel communication to the world. He also exemplified the revival being broadcasted to hundreds of millions of people being saved, healed, and delivered through that Spirit-filled miracle television network.

Amid the dream, I sensed the enemy's attempt to instill fear and intimidation in the world that resulted in splitting the church, forcing them to choose between fear and faith. I was troubled as I watched the events unfolding caused by the faulty foundations of cessation's theology.

Cessationism is the view that the miraculous gifts of the Spirit, such as healing, tongues, and prophetic revelation, pertained to the apostolic era only, served a purpose that was unique to establishing the early church, and passed away before the canon of Scripture was closed. Any honest theologian who understand biblical hermeneutics knows it is n assumption made by biased preachers.

The powerless gospel, created by doubt and corrupted theology, is rampant in the church, and it neuters those who succumb to it. The false gospel prepared a path for a spirit of fear to grip much of the church worldwide, as media influence and fake news propagated the lie of a false pandemic.

There is a Global Glory Revival coming to the airwaves to facilitate the Billion Soul Harvest before the second coming of Jesus, the Messiah. The forces of evil continue to broadcast their distorted diabolical news, while we fight for television and online space to proclaim the message of Christ. Because of the dominant control by secular media, many were duped by the false narrative being broadcast to the world. The millions of people who daily watch the news believe it is all true. If it is on television, it must be true, right? Wrong! The broadcast indoctrination of the masses is creating a severe problem. Satan is known as the Prince of the Power of the air, and his influence is detrimental to God's purposes in this hour. The deception is rampant. Two thousand years ago, Paul addressed Satan's influential power in this present age.

And you [He made alive when you] were [spiritually] dead and separated from Him because of your transgressions and sins, in which you once walked. You were following the ways of this world [influenced by this present age], in accordance with the prince of the power of the air (Satan), the spirit who is now at work in the disobedient [the unbelieving, who fight against the purposes of God]. Among these [unbelievers] we all once lived in the passions of our flesh [our behavior governed by the sinful self-], indulging the desires of [a]human nature [without the Holy Spirit] and [the impulses] of the [sinful] mind. We were, by nature, children [under the sentence] of [God's] wrath, just like the rest [of mankind]. But God, being [so very] rich in mercy, because of His great and wonderful love with which He loved us, even when we were [spiritually] dead and separated from Him because of our sins, He made us [spiritually] alive together with Christ (for by His grace—His undeserved favor and mercy—you have been saved from God's judgment). And He raised us up together with Him [when we believed], and seated us with Him in the heavenly places, [because we are] in Christ Jesus (Ephesians 2:1-6, AMP).

CIVIL WAR IN THE CHURCH

In 2011, my spiritual father, Prophet Bob Jones, also had an encounter concerning this coming Civil War. Here are excerpts from that message.

The Lord began to deal with me on the subject of a coming Civil War in the church. The angel of this nation is called "Union." If you study the prophetic nature of the visions of George Washington, you will see that he is the angel that appeared to him in his darkest hour. Some miraculous things took place with George Washington. While they were in battle, his enemies began to believe that he couldn't be killed because when they shot at him, he would not be hit. They would shoot the horses out from underneath him, but he had the Divine hand on him. I believe that Divine hand is coming again to America, and America is being called to come into a divine union again.

There is coming a Civil War into the church, and every one of you is going to have a civil war inside of you. It will be the Grey matter of the mind, the revel, against the blue matter of the mind, the revelation of the Son of heaven. We have tried to bring unity in our midst for a few hundred years in America. There has not been any unity. There can only be unity when we become united in the Spirit.

There is a remnant of people who are getting ready to come forth like love slaves. Their ear will be fine-tuned to the Master. One of the things God was dealing with me this morning was how much do you want to pray in the Spirit? So, the civil war is getting ready to start, and we are getting prepared for it; the Grey has gone to surrender to the Blue. Do you have any idea what an army in unity can do? You know, there is principalities and powers throughout the dominion, demonic that are reigning over this place right now. Do you know what an army of Blue would do? We'd pull down the principalities. One of you can't do it, a hundred of you can't do it, a thousand of you can't do it, but several churches joining together in unity can. He is calling us to become an army that stays in step with one another, who will not go AWOL or get out of step, marching together in unity, led by the Spirit.[1]

AN ARMY OF UNITY

In his book, *Letter from Birmingham Jail*, Martin Luther King Jr., wrote these poignant words relevant to our times. "In a real sense, all life is inter-related. All men are caught in an inescapable network of mutuality, tied in a single garment of destiny. Whatever affects one directly, affects all indirectly. I can never be what I ought to be until you are what you ought to be, and you can never be what you ought to be until I am what I ought to be. This is the interrelated structure of reality."[2] Unity is critical, but it must be built on a solid foundation. Unity in diversity requires good people to learn how to speak the same thing, with one voice, and be perfectly joined together in Christ. Paul's words are applicable in every generation, but maybe more so in our time.

Now I plead with you, brethren, by the name of our Lord Jesus Christ, that you all speak the same thing, and that there be no divisions among you, but that you be perfectly joined together in the same mind and in the same judgment. [3]

That ye all speak the same thing: To "speak the same thing" stands opposed to speaking conflicting, controversial words. Though perfect uniformity of opinion and doctrine cannot be expected, yet on the great and fundamental doctrines of Christianity, Christians should agree. On all points in which they differ, they may demonstrate peace and love, as long as we don't violate the fundamental truths of the Gospel.

In essentials unity, in non-essentials liberty, in all things, charity. Philip Schaff, the distinguished nineteenth-century church historian, calls this saying "the watchword of Christian peacemakers."

"Often, attributed to great theologians such as Augustine, it comes from an otherwise undistinguished German Lutheran theologian of the early seventeenth century, Rupertus Meldenius. The phrase occurs in a tract on Christian unity written (circa 1627) during the Thirty Year War (1618–1648), a bloody time in European history in which religious tensions played a significant role." [4]

And that there be no divisions among you: The Greek word is schismata and is translated as "schisms" and means no divisions created by contending parties and sects. The church was to be regarded as one and indivisible, and not to be torn into different factions and stretched under the banners of diverse leaders.

But that ye be perfectly joined together: The word used here and rendered "perfectly joined together," denotes to restore, mend, to fit or adapt anything to its proper place so that it shall be complete in all its parts, and harmonious. The goal of church leaders is to compose and settle controversies, to produce harmony and order in the body of Christ. The apostle evidently desires the church to be united in feeling; that every member of the church should occupy his appropriate place, as every member of a well-balanced body, or part of a machine, has its proper place and use; see his wishes more fully expressed in 1Co. 12:12-31. [5]

In the same mind: This cannot mean that they were united in precisely the same shades of opinion, which is impossible, but that their minds were to be disposed toward each other with mutual goodwill. The word here rendered "mind," denotes not merely the intellect itself, but that which is in the mind, the thoughts and counsels. [6]

And in the same judgment: This word properly denotes knowledge, opinion, or sentiment, and sometimes, as here, the purpose of the mind, or will. Union of feeling is possible even where people differ much in their views of things. They may love each other much, even where they do not see alike. They may give each other credit for honesty and sincerity and may be willing to suppose that others "may be right," and "honest" even where their views differ. The foundation of Christian union is not so much laid in uniformity of intellectual perception as the right feelings of the heart. And the proper way to produce union in the church of God is not to begin by attempting to equalize all intellects on the bed of theolgians, but to produce supreme love of God, and elevated and pure Christian love to all who bear the image and the name of the Redeemer. [7]

THE NATRUAL MIND VERSUS THE SPIRITUAL MIND

The Civil War, mentioned by Sid Roth and Bob Jones, spoke of divisions and civil unrest. Those disruptions emerged in an atmosphere of conflict between the natural and spiritual mind, and that is the problem in the body of Christ. In too many places, the Christian's discerning capacity has been incapacitated by the natural mind and become incapable of receiving nor discerning the things of the Spirit of God.

> But the natural man does not receive the things of the Spirit of God, for they are foolishness to him; nor can he know them, because they are spiritually discerned. But he who is spiritual judges all things, yet he himself is rightly judged by no one. For "who has known the mind of the Lord that he may instruct Him?" But we have the mind of Christ.[8]

The natural mind is readily influenced by personal and national events, blockading the mind from logical and spiritual thinking. The Covid-19 pandemic assists me in making my case. The pandemic is the culprit that created wide-spread fear, confusion, and government intrusion in the church. Local and state governments endeavored to close the door to the churches or, at least, limit the number of people in church services. The insistence on wearing a mask has been a thorn in the flesh for many people. Most churches adhered to the law of closing the church doors, while some reverted to outdoor church services, and others converted traditional services into online events. When individual states mandated that church could not meet for services, instead of questioning the mandate, they asked, *"How long should we shut our doors."* The church is stuck in the middle of a pandemic war, which generated a spirit of intimidation and fear, while the fake prophetic forecasters overplayed the pandemic narrative. I am not saying that we don't live in a difficult and dangerous time because of Covid-19. What concerns me is the fear that has paralyzed our nation, and the government's intrusion into the church has become a serious issue that needs to be resolved.

I believe much of the church will eventually overcome fear by exercising their faith in God. Re-election of President Donald Trump will lead us to a better, more stable place. Ultimately, we must turn our eyes away from the earthly things and lift our faces towards heaven, as we pray for divine assistance. It is valuable to remind you once again of the 3rd George Washington angelic visitation.

"Son of the Republic, look and learn." When the voice had ceased, the dark shadowy angel placed his trumpet once more to his mouth and blew a long and fearful blast.

When the voice had ceased, the dark shadowy angel placed his trumpet once more to his mouth and blew a long and fearful blast. Instantly a light of a thousand suns shone down from above me and pierced and broke into fragments the dark cloud which enveloped America.

In this third and great "Peril," George Washington saw the dark shadowy angel placing his mouth to the TRUMP that blew a long fearful blast is a prophetic picture of a heavenly agent imposing heaven's will on the dark cloud that now envelops America.

ABRAHAM LINCOLN'S PROCLAMATION

By the President of the United States of America.

A Proclamation.

"Whereas, the Senate of the United States, devoutly recognizing the Supreme Authority and just Government of Almighty God, in all the affairs of men and of nations, has, by a resolution, requested the President to designate and set apart a day for National prayer and humiliation.

And whereas it is the duty of nations as well as of men, to own their dependence upon the overruling power of God, to confess their sins and transgressions, in humble sorrow, yet with assured hope that genuine repentance will lead to mercy and pardon; and to recognize the sublime truth, announced in the Holy Scriptures and proven by all history, that those nations only are blessed whose God is the Lord.

And, insomuch as we know that, by His divine law, nations like individuals are subjected to punishments and chastisements in this world, may we not justly fear that the awful calamity of civil war, which now desolates the land, may be but a punishment, inflicted upon us, for our presumptuous sins, to the needful end of our national reformation as a whole People? We have been the recipients of the choicest bounties of Heaven. We have been preserved, these many years, in peace and prosperity. We have grown in numbers, wealth and power, as no other nation has ever grown. But we have forgotten God. We have forgotten the gracious hand which preserved us in peace, and multiplied and enriched and strengthened us; and we have vainly imagined, in the deceitfulness of our hearts, that all these blessings were produced by some superior wisdom and virtue of our own. Intoxicated with unbroken success, we have become too self-sufficient to feel the necessity of redeeming and preserving grace, too proud to pray to the God that made us!

It behooves us then, to humble ourselves before the offended Power, to confess our national sins, and to pray for clemency and forgiveness.

Now, therefore, in compliance with the request, and fully concurring in the views of the Senate, I do, by this my proclamation, designate and set apart Thursday, the 30th. day of April 1863, as a day of national humiliation, fasting and prayer. And I do hereby request all the People to abstain, on that day, from their ordinary secular pursuits, and to unite, at their several places of public worship and their respective homes, in keeping the day holy to the Lord, and devoted to the humble discharge of the religious duties proper to that solemn occasion.

All this being done, in sincerity and truth, let us then rest humbly in the hope authorized by the Divine teachings, that the united cry of the Nation will be heard on high, and answered with blessings, no less than the pardon of our national sins, and the restoration of our now divided and suffering Country, to its former happy condition of unity and peace.

In witness whereof, I have hereunto set my hand and caused the seal of the United States to be affixed.

Done at the City of Washington, this thirtieth day of March, in the year of our Lord one thousand eight hundred and sixty-three, and of the Independence of the United States the eighty seventh." [9]

By the President: Abraham Lincoln

7

LADY LIBERTY'S FREEDOM TORCH

AND THE RISE OF THE POWER PURITY PROPHETS

I have seen the Power Purity Prophets rising with incredible power and love to bring in the great harvest before the second coming of Jesus Christ. Bob Jones called them "a harvest of harvesters." The harvest is ready, but the laborers are few. However, in these days, God has sent His messengers to recruit a company of harvesters for the end-time revival.

The book of Ezekiel chapter 44 speaks of the Zadok priesthood that would teach the people the difference between the clean and the unclean, and between the holy and the profane.

"The priests shall teach My people the difference between the holy and the common, and teach them to distinguish between the (ceremonially) unclean and the clean." [1]

The Power Purity Prophets will teach people the difference between the holy and profane and will enable them to "discern between the unclean and the clean." Once the people are taught the difference between holy and profane, they can cultivate their ability to discern.

The book of Malachi speaks about the pure sons of Levi who are actually a forerunning breed of ministries that is likened unto the "spirit of Elijah"

> "Behold, I am going to send My messenger, and he will prepare and clear the way before Me. And the Lord [the Messiah], whom you seek, will suddenly come to His temple; the Messenger of the covenant, in whom you delight, behold, He is coming," says the Lord of hosts. But who can endure the day of His coming? And who can stand when He appears? For He is like a refiner's fire and like launderer's soap [which removes impurities and uncleanness]. He will sit as a refiner and purifier of silver, and He will purify the sons of Levi [the priests], and refine them like gold and silver, so that they may present to the Lord [grain] offerings in righteousness. [2]

These purified prophets belong to the Lord and show themselves as a type of John the Baptist and Elijah. They will teach the difference between right and wrong and the power of purity. Their God is a refiner's fire, and that makes all the difference. A refiner's fire does not destroy indiscriminately like a forest fire. A refiner's fire does not consume completely like the fire of an incinerator. A refiner's fire refines. It purifies and makes people ready for the day of the Lord, the day of harvest.

> Then those who feared the Lord [with awe-filled reverence] spoke to one another; and the Lord paid attention and heard it,

and a book of remembrance was written before Him of those who fear the Lord [with an attitude of reverence and respect] and who esteem His name. "They will be Mine," says the Lord of hosts, "on that day when I publicly recognize them and openly declare them to be My own possession [that is, My very special treasure]. And I will have compassion on them and spare them as a man spares his own son who serves him." Then you will again distinguish between the righteous and the wicked, between the one who serves God and the one who does not serve Him.[3]

The Purity Power Prophets are rising with incredible authority and glory, stemming from intimate union with Jesus Christ. They will carry fire and anointing that will shake nations, and they will stand before presidents and kings, delivering the Word of the Lord with deadly precision and accuracy. It's time for the fires of "revival reformation" to sweep the nations again, and I believe it's knocking at the door.

"But for you who fear My name [with awe-filled reverence] the sun of righteousness will rise with healing in its wings. And you will go forward and leap [joyfully] like calves [released] from the stall. You will trample the wicked, for they will be ashes under the soles of your feet on the day that I do this," says the Lord of hosts. "Remember [with thoughtful concern] the Law of Moses My servant, the statutes and the ordinances which I commanded him on [Mount] Horeb [to give] to all Israel."

"Behold, I am going to send you Elijah the prophet before the coming of the great and terrible day of the Lord. He will turn the hearts of the fathers to their children, and the hearts of the children to their fathers [a reconciliation produced by repentance], so that I will not come and strike the land with a curse [of complete destruction]."[4]

"These are the days of Elijah declaring the word of the Lord. And these are the days of Your servant, Moses, righteousness being restored. These are the days of the harvest and the fields are all white in the world. And we are the laborers that are in your vineyard, declaring the Word of the Lord. There is no God like Jeohovah."[5]

A NEW PROPHETIC EAGLE HAS ARRIVED

The Lord spoke to me about a *new harvesting eagle* that is being released in this season that will play a significant role in bringing in the billion-soul harvest that Bob Jones saw in 1977. The Lord said that the world has never seen this type of eagle before and that it is "Spiritually Ambidextrous," which means that this brand of prophets is a combination of the Seer and Nabi Prophet and the devil has no remedy or answer for them. In Hebrew, *Nabi* means *to bubble forth, as from a fountain.* The Nabi prophets were ones who announced or poured forth the declarations of God. A seer was a prophet who saw visions— pictures or scenes seen in visions, dreams, or the natural eye.

The Lord showed me that before the second coming of Jesus Christ this new prophetic eagle or people will be operating in full prophetic capacity and anointed in power to bring in the great harvest. Just as John the Baptist came to prepare the coming of the Lord, so this new eagle will be an Elijah Company turning the hearts of God's people back to God as did John and Elijah.

BEHOLD I WILL SEND YOU ELIJAH

To fully understand what this looks like, let's review what the Scripture writes concerning John the Baptist. The Scriptures tell us that Zechariah and Elizabeth had no child and were crying out to God. They wondered if God would ever answer their prayer. One day, Zechariah was serving in the temple, burning incense when Gabriel appeared to him (see Luke 1:11-17 AMP).

The angel Gabriel quoted what was written of Elijah in the book of Malachi 4:4-6. The prophet Malachi prophesied that before the Lord comes, that God would send Elijah the prophet to turn the Father's hearts to the children and the children to their fathers. It is exactly what Elijah did in 1 Kings 18.

THE SPIRIT AND POWER OF ELIJAH

Elijah approached all the people and said, "How long will you hesitate between two opinions? If the Lord is God, follow Him; but if Baal, follow him." [6]

Through signs and wonders, Elijah revealed to the people that, "The Lord, He is God" and all Israel repented and turned back toward God (see 1 Kings 18:36-39). This was the prophetic task that John the Baptist and Elijah fulfilled. John accomplished his calling as a voice, "Crying in the Wilderness" and then "Prepared the way of the Lord making the path straight." (see Mark 1:3). Elijah's voice was a different voice compared to the Baptist. His voice was reflected in a question and a command. "How long will you be between two opinions? Choose today who you will serve!"

JESUS, MOSES AND ELIJAH ON THE MOUNT OF TRANSFIGURATION

"After six days Jesus took with him Peter and James and John, and led them up a high mountain by themselves. And he was transfigured before them.[7] The Transfiguration was the singular event where Jesus appeared in radiant glory on the mountain, accompanied by Moses and Elijah. In the transfiguration, Moses and Elijah's presence was recognized as summarizing "the Law and the Prophets" now being fulfilled in and by Jesus' life. Moses is obviously representing the Law, while Elijah represented the prophets. Both went up mountains and encoutered the fiery majesty of the Lord, Moses on Mount Sinai, and Elijah on Mount Carmel.

> And as they were going down the mountain, Jesus commanded them, "Do not tell anyone what you have seen until the Son of Man has been raised from the dead." The disciples asked Him, "Then why do the scribes say that Elijah must come first?" He answered and said, "Elijah is coming and will restore all things; but I say to you that Elijah has come already, and they did not recognize him, but did to him as they wished. The Son of Man is also going to suffer at their hands."

Then the disciples understood that He had spoken to them about John the Baptist. Matthew 17:9-13

Notice what Jesus said. *"Elijah IS coming and WILL restore all things."* (verse 12, emphasis added). Then, He said, *"Elijah has come already."* (verse 12). The verses regarding Elijah are two separate people, the forerunner, and the Messiah. The fact that *Elijah has already come* refers to John the Baptist, who was the forerunner of the coming Messiah and the *Elijah is coming refers* to Christ the Messiah who will restore all things. The coming Elijah is also the Elijah company that will assist in Christ's restorative work.

Elijah came on the scene before the first coming of Jesus Christ, then in the second coming of Jesus there will be an "Elijah Company" who comes to prepare the way of the Lord and to turn the hearts of the people back to God, through the spirit of revival. The Elijah Company will restore the hearts of the people during a time of revival, as they move in the spirit and the power of Elijah, as prophesied by Gabriel.

Elijah does not come this time as an individual, but rather as a corporately anointed body of believers invading the earth with signs and wonders and shifting nations an outpouring of the Holy Spirit that will bring in the billion-soul harvest.

BOB JONES SAW THE ARMY OF GOD IN 1979

In 1979, Bob Jones saw an army that would come in two stages. The first stage would be a wave of leaders that would raise the greatest army that nothing could stop." The Lord told Bob: "I will release them in power, and I will arm them from My armory in heaven. There is no gift I will deny them. They will pull down the warehouses of God filled with spiritual food to feed the nations, and they will have no fear of the enemy. They will glorify Him beyond anything that has ever been seen. They will represent Him in His holiness and compassion."

This Elijah Company is hungry for the glorious presence of God. Unlike this company, prior generations were bound, with the "rules and regulations" that have crippled, stunted or killed the post-modern church. This army of God only desires one thing, the kingdom of power and glory.

When we begin to see heavenly outpourings happening in the United States and the other nations, then a new prophetic voice will sound, proclaiming the word of the Lord, as John the Baptist and Elijah did, calling for a return to the living God. This prophetic company will move in signs, wonders and miracles and be the voice of one crying in the nations that will be heard.

KING DAVID'S DREAD CHAMPIONS

The men and women of these days will, in many ways, be like King David's mighty men. They will stand in unlikely places and move with supernatural power, unlike what the world has ever seen. Society won't know what to do with them. Many of these champions will be unknown on earth, but they will be known in heaven. The presence of God will be their secret strength. They are the wild ones, no hold's barred, no risk too great, no prize too small, and if He says it, they will do it. The dread champions will challenge the masses with zeal too bright to contain, passion too great to fit into the boxes and walls of churches built with small- minded dreams, and not fortresses of kingdom expan-

LADY LIBERTY'S FREEDOM TORCH | 83

sion. They are busting through the resistance, breakers and shakers, prophets and preachers, evangelists and singers, that have lost sight of the world and only see Him.[8]

> But the LORD is with me like a dread champion; therefore, my persecutors will stumble and not prevail. They will be utterly ashamed, because they have failed.[9]

A clarion call to the church in this season is mandated by heaven and sounded by the angels, urging the church to rise from slumber to a glorious place of the supernatural miracles of Jesus. Get ready, there is a great harvest of souls coming, and this harvest will be brought in by a supernatural generation that has been carefully prepared for harvest. This many-membered, corporately anointed, Body of Christ will do the same miracles Jesus did 2,000 years ago—and greater works will they do. We are His Body, and Christ will reap the reward of His suffering. The Lord will roar out of Zion, and the harvest will come. I believe we are the generation of harvest, and now is the time to reap what has been sown.

LADY LIBERTY'S FLAME WILL NOT GO OUT

"The tallest lady in America is 151 feet tall plus one inch. Her name is Lady Liberty. She has stood for over 130 years as an icon of freedom, her torch a beacon of hope. But as British philosopher John Locke poignantly edified, there is no freedom without the LAW: The end of law is not to abolish or restrain, but to preserve and enlarge freedom." [10]

Lady Liberty represents freedom from persecution by the

government, freedom from social and economic oppression, and even freedom of religious beliefs and practices. This majestic "lady" is an emblem of the personal liberty upon which our country was built. The iconic torch represents the fire of God's love and power symbolic of the Holy Spirit in this nation as we proudly recite the banner on our currency, *"In God We Trust."*

From this time forward into the second term of Trump's administration, darkness will continue to be exposed at the highest level for all the world to see. There will be equal justice under the law as Lady Liberty continues to proudly extend the torch of freedom in her right hand. demanding the equality of liberty and justice for all.

"If God is for us, who can be against us?" That was the question the apostle Paul asked in his letter to the Romans. [11]God's favor, love, and grace trump everything because there is no one or nothing greater than God. There is nothing greater nor more powerful than Jehovah. This is not a promise of the absence of resistance. Instead, it is a promise regarding the impotence of opposition. God will vanquish every enemy that rises up against us. Stand still and see the salvation of the Lord.

As heaven intervened and fought for Israel's expulsion from Egyptian captivity, the God of America will again supernaturally defend the Union. This is a time of cleansing in America. The dark clouds witnessed by Washington in his epic angelic encounter will be displaced and dispersed by the blast of the TRUMP.

And just when it seems all hope is lost, *the "TRUMP will Sound" and Instantly the light of a thousand suns will shine down from above, and pierce and break into fragments the dark cloud that is now enveloping America.*

A new era will be ushered in and a time of healing will occur in America, made possible by our Father. Again, I remind you that the light of a thousand suns of angels will push back darkness and establish the banner of our true American destiny with its promises of a renewed America. Once again, Lady Liberty will proudly extend her flaming torch into the skies as a sign to foreigners and immigrants that they are welcome to our shores.

In a park at the base of Miss Liberty is a statue of a woman named, Emma Lazarus, who's famous 1883 sonnet *"The New Colossus"* sits in bronze at her feet.

Not like the brazen giant of Greek fame,
With conquering limbs astride from land to land;
Here at our sea-washed, sunset gates shall stand
A mighty woman with a torch, whose flame
Is the imprisoned lightning, and her name
Mother of Exiles. From her beacon-hand
Glows world-wide welcome; her mild eyes command
The air-bridged harbor that twin cities frame.
"Keep, ancient lands, your storied pomp!" cries she
With silent lips. "Give me your tired, your poor,
Your huddled masses yearning to breathe free,
The wretched refuse of your teeming shore.
Send these, the homeless, tempest-tossed to me,
I lift my lamp beside the door!"[12]

It's been said over and over again: freedom isn't free. The reason we can enjoy freedom is that someone was responsible. Leaders led. People worked. Soldiers fought. Many died. Freedom came with a price. In a summary statement, freedom requires responsibility. Freedom and responsibility always go together.

We must never give away the freedom attained by the cost of great sacrifice. Don't forget the words of Benjamin Franklin, "Any society that would give up a little liberty to gain a little security will deserve neither and lose both."

We are forever indebted to those who gave their lives for our freedom in the Revolutionary War and afterward.

8

THE LAST TRUMP, THE DESTINY OF GOD'S AMERICA

We shall not all sleep, but we will be changed, in a moment, in the twinkling of an eye, at the last trump: for the trumpet shall sound, and the dead shall be raised incorruptible, and we shall be changed.[1]

"Unconventional" describes Trump from the beginning. Trump is a real estate tycoon with TV celebrity status but no official political experience in running for or serving in local or state government. With his celebrity status, charismatic personality, demeanor, organizational skill, rhetorical skill, and personal wealth, he miraculously managed to win an election.

He became president of the United States against all the odds. He fought the Republican establishment and won, fought the Democratic establishment and won, and now is in a battle with the establishment media and Deep State and hopes to win again in 2020. Time for the Trumpet to sound.

"Son of the Republic, look and learn." When the voice had ceased,

the dark shadowy angel placed his trumpet once more to his mouth and blew a long and fearful blast.

When the voice had ceased, the dark shadowy angel placed his trumpet once more to his mouth and blew a long and fearful blast. Instantly a light of a thousand suns shone down from above me and pierced and broke into fragments the dark cloud which enveloped America.

A TRUMP VICTORY

Once again, I reiterate, there is not a doubt in my mind, President TRUMP will secure a second term as President. When he is elected to his second term, the blast of the TRUMP will dishearten the principalities of the dark cloud with the red eyes. Many will fall from grace due to exposure of corruption and wrongdoing as angel forces are released from heaven. Like the light of a thousand suns shining down, it will pierce and break into fragments the dark cloud that has enveloped America.

"Trump continues to fight against the establishment by trying to secure borders, trying to withdraw military forces from abroad such as from Syria and Afghanistan, trying to create friendly relationships with Russia and North Korea, imposing tariffs and trying to cure a massive trade imbalance with nations such as China, trying to get nuclear and military behavioral concessions from Iran, trying to get other nations to pay more for United States military presence abroad, cutting corporate taxes and trying to get companies to invest more in the United States, and generally trying to regain what greatness the United States had historically.

There is no doubt that Trump is an unconventional maverick

who is not going to change much while in office. Being very different is something the status quo establishment isn't very fond of. Judging by the disarray among the Democratic candidates for president, it seems on the surface that Trump has succeeded in singlehandedly destroying the Democratic leadership."[2]

This last election showed people that analyst who participate on celebrated news networks like CNN, MSNBC, FOX News, ABC, New York Times, Washington Post and other mainstream media networks are not too knowledgeable about political predictions. The pseudo pundits called to feed the propaganda of liberal media for the most part lack common sense. It also shows that polls conducted by liberal mainstream media networks are ridiculous and fallacious.

In an opinion article on Fox News website, Newt Gingrich shared his perspective about the upcoming election. "Biden is in the Dewey spring and summer period of a soft lead, with no real campaign. Furthermore, like all left-wingers, Biden has the enormous advantage that the news media will do everything it can to weaken President Trump and protect the presumptive Democratic nominee.

President Trump also has the advantage of endurance, which is captured in his book, The Art of the Comeback. He knows what it is like to be virtually bankrupt, exhausted, with no obvious way forward, and still force success through intelligence and hard work."[3]

Patriotism, the love of God and country, and conservatism will ignite passion in the Union, the closer we get to the election. The Patriots will come out of the woodwork when Americans shift from the Covid-19 pandemic, and they will take a stand against the radical left-wing ideology. Love of life, liberty and God, and country will lead to the dispersing and exposing of the Deep State nefarious underground activity, including trafficking and unthinkable evil and corruption. Many will be exposed as traitors of the Union, as hidden schemes of darkness come to light.

DIVINE INTERVENTION

As it happened with General George Washington at Valley Forge, there will be another divine intervention as the *"GOD OF AMERICA"* overthrows cowardly corrupt systems and the deception propagated by the media. These dark practitioners of evil have secretly stolen and offered up the pure and guiltless to feed the evil entities with the blood of innocent children from legalized abortion to the abduction, sale, trafficking, and sacrifice of the more than 800,000 innocent children that go missing in this nation every year.

Snatching victory from the jaws of defeat, in the end, God will win the last battle.

These satanic practitioners and the propagators of evil will be exposed from Wall Street to Washington and everything in between for all to see as the *"GOD OF AMERICA"* fights for the innocence of a nation whose freedom and future are at stake. God will intervene and save the nation.

Outspoken conservative rocker Ted Nugent was the featured guest on the May 21 edition of the show, "Triggered," hosted by President Trump's eldest son, Donald Trump, Jr. This is one piece of their conversation.

"He's on a mission from God," Ted added. "This is divine

intervention. We needed a status quo crusher, and I can't think of anybody except Donald J. Trump that could have pulled it off with such effectiveness, such absolutism and shall I say, aplomb (self-confidence). I think we can all learn lessons from your dad."[4]

IF GOD IS FOR US, WHO CAN BE AGAINST US

God has blessed us in America far beyond what we can ever imagine. I wonder if this generation has any concept of the part the sovereign God of the universe played in the founding and sustaining of our country. Many of us are not feeling good about America these days. We have serious questions about our nation's future.,

The big question remains. Is God really for us as a nation? I say yes, thousand times, yes. At least that was true in the early days of our founding. But if we continue to go our own foolish way, how long will God be patient before His full judgment is exerted?

In today's political world, the terms "Make America Great Again" and "Keep America Great" are focused on the greatness of our country. But do we know the truth about the source of America's greatness? We tend to think it's our superior military power and the richness of our affluence and financial blessings. The truth is God's sovereign, providential hand has been at work since our country's very beginning. America's greatness is more dependent upon God than its military might, as great as it is.

In 1492 Columbus came seeking the favor and will of God. He named his first landing, San Salvador, which means Christ the Savior, or Holy Savior. The pilgrims came to live in freedom and to express their faith and founding on Christian principles. Our Declaration of Independence that took place in 1776 and our Constitution which was signed in 1787, as well as the Bill of Rights, all presumed a religious order based on Christ Jesus as their cornerstone and building block. To assume it was a secular state is to misread the history of the founding of the nation. Under the guiding hand of our sovereign God, our Constitution was designed to perpetuate a Christian order. Everything about our founding government was based on both the Old Testament and New Testament principles of ethics and morality.

The First Amendment prohibits the forming of a state religion, such as was the Church of England. But at the same time, there were no restrictions on our freedom to exercise personal religious beliefs, whether Christian or otherwise. The idea of separation of church and state is nowhere to be found in the Constitution. Never in their wildest imaginations did our Founding Fathers conceive of a time when our boys and girls would be forbidden to pray in public schools, at graduation exercises, and football games. Never did they have in mind divorcing God and government, nor reading the Bible in public schools. In fact, it is widely known that the Bible was the very first and only textbook in the first schools in America.

Charles Malic, a citizen of Lebanon and onetime representative to the United Nations from Lebanon, articulated these words. *"The good in the United States would never come into being without the blessing of Jesus Christ." If God is for us, who can be against us?"*[5]

Whatever some politicians may think, the irrefutable truth is that America's soul is at best and highest Christian. In a radio sermon by Pastor Jack Graham (recorded some 20 plus years ago), I heard him say that yes, America does have a soul that was for God, and was made to know God and experience Him. But according to Billy Graham, *"America is in danger of losing her soul."* He emphasized that America did not happen by chance. God guided the hands, minds, and the eyes of our forefathers and our nation. His sovereign hand shaped the very fabric of our nation and the freedom we enjoy.

Jesus's words have rung true in every generation. *"You shall know the Truth and the Truth shall make you free"* (John 8:32)

I submit that no government can give freedom. The government can protect freedom and preserve freedom, but only God is the Author of all liberty and freedom, and only He can give freedom. Fifty of the 56 signers of the Declaration of Independence were God-fearing men who considered themselves born again Christians. A similar number of the original constitutionalists were bold Christians, active in the service of Jesus Christ.

James Madison, our fourth president, was clear where he stood as far as the founding principle of government. *"We have staked the whole future of American civilization not on the power of government, far from it, but on the Ten Commandments of God."* [6]

Andrew Johnson, our 17th president, echoed the words of Madison. *"Our republic rests on the Rock of Scripture."* [7]

President Reagan used *his* remarks at the 1983 Prayer Breakfast to announce his *Proclamation of the Year of the Bible.* Clearly, the participants at that long-ago breakfast were happy to hear this good news. Just as clearly, the cultured despisers of religion were unhappy. It was too much mixing of church and state to their taste. Even so, President Reagan held firm. He never wavered in declaring that *"The Old and New Testaments of the*

Bible inspired many of the early settlers of our country, providing them with the strength, character, convictions, and faith necessary to withstand great hardship and danger in this new and rugged land."[8]

Given our rapid decline and falling away from our founding Christian principles, maybe a more realistic statement would be, *"If God is against us who can be for us."* Mr. Graham said in effect that the day America decides that we don't need God, and the principles of the Bible, and that we no longer commit ourselves to follow Christ and the Word of God, that is the day America begins to die. The question for all Americans to consider is not if God is on our side, but rather, are we on God's side?

"For what will it profit a man [or nation] if he gains the whole world, and loses his soul?" [9]

Let's remember, and renew our commitment to the founding principles of our forefathers: The sanctity of human life, the value and dignity of the human soul, monogamous family, common decency and truthfulness, the value of the work ethic, our general freedom to own land, the principle of less government control, and our God-given right to life, liberty, and the pursuit of happiness. "If God be for us, who can be against us?"

9

FOR SUCH A TIME AS THIS

I n 1517, power was in the hands of the few, thought was controlled by the chosen, and common people lived lives without hope. When Martin Luther nailed his 95 Theses to the door of Castle Church in Wittenberg, there was a great need for reformation. On October 31 of that year, a penniless monk sparked the revolution that would change everything.

The spark became a flame that engulfed the church's corrupted institution and brought forth the Protestant Reformation. In defiance of the current Pontiff, Luther began his famous document simply saying, "Out of love for the truth and the desire to bring it to light, the following propositions will be discussed at Wittenberg, under the presidency of the Reverend Father Martin Luther." He had no army, but this Reformation movement changed the Western culture generating the drive towards freedom of religion and the separation of church and state. Without the Reformation, there would be no pilgrims, no puritans, and no America the way we know it. The right words, combined with courageous action, can become a watershed moment.

Words spoken at a momentous time and actions taken at a critical moment will echo through time because of the stirring they caused both then and now —words and actions matter. Ask any coach who has given a pep talk at halftime. Ask the military leader on the eve of battle. Politicians know it. So do pastors, lawyers, and salespeople. Words must be transformed into action. Words followed by action makes all the difference.

Words have energy and power with the ability to help, to heal, and to change the heart. Abraham Heschel, a Jewish leader during the civil rights movement, often spoke concerning the power of words. Speech has power. Words do not fade. What starts as a sound, ends in a deed."

"Ask not what your country can do for you. Ask what you can do for your country." (John F. Kennedy)

"Let us therefore brace ourselves to our duties, and so bear ourselves that if the British Empire and its Commonwealth last for a thousand years, men will still say, 'This was their finest hour.'" (Winston Churchill)

"I have a dream that one day every valley shall be exalted, and every hill and mountain shall be made low, the rough places will be made plain, and the crooked places will be made straight, and the glory of the Lord shall be revealed and all flesh shall see it together. We will be able to hew out of the mountain of despair a stone of hope." (Martin Luther King, Jr.)[1]

"You come to me with a sword, with a spear, and with a javelin. But I come to you in the name of the Lord of hosts, the God of the armies of Israel, whom you have defied." (King David)

It would unforgiveable if we did not remember that great speech Abraham Lincoln delivered at Gettysburg.

THE GETTYSBURG ADDRESS

Finally, there's Abraham Lincoln's Gettysburg Address, given in 1863 at the dedication of the Union cemetery at the Gettysburg battlefield. This has become one of the most famous speeches in American history. It is so brilliantly brief that countless American schoolchildren have memorized it. But Lincoln was not even the featured speaker at Gettysburg that day. That role fell to Edward Everett, a former congressman and Harvard president who was probably the nation's most celebrated orator in 1863. Everett gave a two-hour long speech that was probably well received, but which is now almost totally ignored.

No one expected Lincoln's two-minute remarks to change the meaning of the war and American history. Before the Gettysburg Address, many white Americans – including northerners – did not wish to extend the blessings of liberty to African Americans. But Lincoln insisted that the Declaration of Independence had founded a nation "conceived in liberty and dedicated to the proposition that all men are created equal."

"Under God," he proclaimed, America would have "a new birth of freedom." His audience would have instantly understood what Lincoln meant. Because of the Civil War, America itself could be "born again," as the Gospel of John puts it, into a new life of freedom: freedom for slaves. Moreover, he believed that the Union army's victory would ensure that "government by the people, of the people, and for the people shall not perish from the earth."

We should rightly remember these people. But we should also remember that they were (or are) ordinary human beings, who made a choice.[2]

Amid a much-contested Civil War, President Abraham Lincoln saw a rebirth of freedom, of the people, by the people and for the people. He understood that a truly free America would mean freedom and equality for every person under the flag. Lincoln's Gettysburg address is one of the most famous speeches ever given. It is stunning in its brevity: ten sentences—272 words—and delivered in just over two minutes...few have said more with less.

Lincoln goes back in time—not the signing of the Constitution, but to the Declaration of Independence. In forming our government, the Constitution was the product of many compromises, most notably, slavery. In contrast, the Declaration of Independence declares our enduring national values. In one sentence, Lincoln summarizes the American project: liberty for all and equality of all.

Lincoln's assertion is two-fold. First, the United States is unique. No nation was ever founded on a commitment to liberty and equality. And the Civil War was a trial to see if a nation based on such lofty ideals could survive.

Lincoln was not in Gettysburg to celebrate the Union victory. Rather, he explains that those who fought were the loyal guardians of the American Experiment. With their blood, they watered the tree of liberty. As Lincoln himself knew, how could his words ever compare to that sacrifice?

Ironically, the world remembers what our sixteenth president said, but do we remember the actions of those who fought at Gettysburg?

Those who fought and died shouldered our nation's enduring values through the refining fire of Gettysburg and the Civil War. Lincoln points to them and challenges the living. Are we prepared to heed their example to do what is necessary to advance the founding ideals of the Declaration of Independence?

The Constitution of the Union was tested during the Civil War. Slavery ended. And with it, the values of liberty and equality were given a "new birth."

However, the struggle for liberty and equality continued... and persists today. Lincoln foresaw this. To remain a nation; "Dedicated to the proposition that all men are created equal" and that, "Government of, by, and for the people shall not perish from the earth" these are the "unfinished work" and the "great task remaining" of every generation.

"Four score and seven years ago, our fathers brought forth on this continent a new nation: conceived in liberty and dedicated to the proposition that all men are created equal.

Now we are engaged in a great civil war. . .testing whether that nation, or any nation so conceived and so dedicated. . . can long endure.

We are met on a great battlefield of that war. We have come to dedicate a portion of that field as a final resting place for those who here gave their lives that that nation might live. It is altogether fitting and proper that we should do this.

But, in a larger sense, we cannot dedicate...we cannot consecrate. . . we cannot hallow this ground. The brave men, living and dead, who struggled here have consecrated it, far above our poor power to add or detract. The world will little note, nor long remember, what we say here, but it can never forget what they did here. It is for us the living, rather, to be dedicated here to the unfinished work which they who fought here have thus far so nobly advanced.

It is rather for us to be here dedicated to the great task remaining before us. . .that from these honored dead we take increased devotion to that cause for which they gave the last full measure of devotion. . . that we here highly resolve that these dead shall not have died in vain. . . that this nation, under God, shall have a new birth of freedom. . . and that government of the people. . .by the people. . .for the people. . . shall not perish from the earth."[3]

PRAYER SAVES A NATION

Whenever God moves, He moves in a situation to bring order where there was confusion. He brings structure where there was chaos. The Tower of Babel divided us; the power of God unites us. What Babel scattered Pentecost gathered. It gathered them together in one place with one accord and suddenly, they had power. Throughout history, individual acts of defiance have proved to be incredibly powerful. It takes courage to stand alone, but brave individuals often galvanized the movements of people who come together and change the world.

Looking through the pages of history, there are people who have been inspired to stir up waves of change, in large ways and small. Look around you in our modern world, and again there, everywhere, are more examples. They are that particular slice of humanity that cannot stand to leave things the way they found them. They seem to understand that to make a difference; they have to be different. By their actions, they create waves of change that roll through the pages of time. They made a difference.

Two people in the Old Testament made a difference. For such a time as this, in a desperate moment surrounded by enemies, they became strong in their weakness and changed the course of a nation. One was a king, and the other was a queen. King Hezekiah and Queen Esther saved a nation. They lived in different times, but their story is our story. We live in times such as theirs.

While fasting is a private discipline that yields many personal benefits, the promises of fasting can also impact your family, your community, and your nation. In the Old Testament, there are two stories where prayer and fasting changed history and saved a nation.

Prayer and faith were the keys to King Hezekiah surviving two life challenging situations, the Assyrian army campaign against Israel and his impending death towards the end of his life. His life testifies to the power of prayer in times of national and personal crisis.

King Hezekiah succeeded his father, wicked King Ahaz, and his first action was to 'clean the swamp.' He wasted no time. He took a harsh stand against his predecessor, who shamefully closed the temple, stopped worshiping the Lord, and promoted idolatry, including offering child sacrifice. Ahaz had led the nation of Judah far astray; Hezekiah led them back to God.

In his radical reforms, he cleansed, restored and reopened

the temple, restarted worship at the temple led by the priests and Levites, and demolished the sites of idol worship. He turned Judah back to the Lord—in a matter of weeks! It's a testimony to *the power of leadership and the influence of one.*

Having finished these reforms, Hezekiah had a crisis on his hands. He had become a thorn in the side of Sennacherib, king of Assyria. Assyria was a much more powerful nation, but Hezekiah's prayer life saved them from their enemies. He called these commanders together and spoke to them. This was one of those watershed speeches that greatly impacted Judah's history. The speech reminded them of the truth. The innumerable hoard of Assyrians was dwarfed by the number on Judah's side because God fought for them. The mighty arm of Assyrian flesh was no match for the power of God.

> Then Hezekiah prayed before the Lord, and said: "O Lord God of Israel, the One who dwells between the cherubim, You are God, You alone, of all the kingdoms of the earth. You have made heaven and earth. Incline Your ear, O Lord, and hear; open Your eyes, O Lord, and see; and hear the words of Sennacherib, which he has sent to reproach the living God. Truly, Lord, the kings of Assyria have laid waste the nations and their lands and have cast their gods into the fire; for they were not gods, but the work of men's hands—wood and stone. Therefore, they destroyed them. Now therefore, O Lord our God, I pray, save us from his hand, that all the kingdoms of the earth may know that You are the Lord God, You alone."[4]

Often, the prophets had to be the voice of the conscience of a king and nation. In this case, king and prophet, Hezekiah and Isaiah, stood together. Hezekiah prayed and Isaiah followed up with the prophetic word of the Lord proclaiming Yahweh's coming victory over the enemies of Israel. The angel of the Lord killed 185,000 Assyrians, forcing Sennacherib to retreat.

This is God's word spoken by Isaiah, the prophet of the Lord.

Therefore, thus says the Lord concerning the king of Assyria:
'He shall not come into this city,
Nor shoot an arrow there,
Nor come before it with shield,
Nor build a siege mound against it.
Says the Lord.
'For I will defend this city, to save it
For My own sake and for My servant David's sake.'[5]

Towards the end of his life, Hezekiah got sick, and the Lord sent the prophet Isaiah to him, saying "Thus says the Lord: 'Set your house in order, for you shall die, and not live'" (Isaiah 38:1). But when Hezekiah heard the prediction, he set his face to the wall and prayed to the Lord asking for healing: "Remember now, O Lord, I pray, how I have walked before You in truth and with a loyal heart, and have done what was good in Your sight. And Hezekiah wept bitterly (2 Kings 20:3).

God heard Hezekiah's prayer and sent Isaiah with a message saying, "I have heard your prayer, I have seen your tears; surely I will heal you... And I will add to your days fifteen years" (2 Kings 20:5,6).

72 HOURS THAT SAVED THE JEWS

In the book of Esther, the Jews were on the verge of destruction because of Haman's evil conspiracy, one of the king's advisors. Haman was filled with wrath against a Jew named Mordecai because he did not 'bow or pay homage.' He sought to destroy all the Jews (Esther 3:5, 6). When Mordecai heard about the edict to annihilate the Jews, he tore his clothes and put on sackcloth and ashes. This is a little odd for us to think about, but this was a way to show the most profound grief they were experiencing.

Mordecai sought help form Queen Esther, who was his niece. Mordecai's request meant Esther would have to risk her life for it was dangerous for her to approach the king without summoned first. So, Esther called a fast. "If you keep quiet at a time like this.... you and your relatives will die. Who knows if perhaps you were made queen for just such a time as this?" Esther prayed, repented and fasted and changed the heart of the king. (Esther 4:16)

Those 72 hours of fasting changed the history of the world. When Esther approached the king on behalf of her people, they became a nation not of defeat, annihilation, suffering, and shame, but a nation of favor. They receive honor and promotion, all because of three days of fasting and prayer.[6]

Mordecai's words to Esther are a clarion call to our generation. *"For if you remain completely silent at this time, relief and deliverance will arise for the Jews from another place, but you and your father's house will perish. Yet who knows whether you have come to the kingdom for such a time as this?"* [7]

We must pray for President Donald Trump and his administration. We must appeal to heaven on behalf of this election to assure that we can secure the future of American values. You and I can help change the history of our nation through prayer and fasting. Prayer is the first step toward victory. It is the step Esther and Mordecai took. It is the step many men and women throughout the pages of Scripture have taken when everyone and everything seemed against them. It is our time to stand up for what is right according to Biblical standards in our church, in our families, in our neighborhoods, in our city, in our state, in our nation.

We are looking at a time that might be the great end-time outpouring and it can only come though prayer and fasting.

Consecrate a fast, Call a sacred assembly; Gather the elders And all the inhabitants of the land Into the house of the LORD your God, And cry out to the LORD.[8]

NATIONAL DAY OF PRAYER

In the midst of these trying and unprecedented times, we are reminded that just as those before us turned to God in their darkest hours, so must we seek His wisdom, strength, and healing hand. We pray that He comforts those who have lost loved ones, heals those who are sick, strengthens those on the front lines, and reassures all Americans that through trust in Him, we can overcome all obstacles.

May we never forget that prayer guides and empowers our Nation and that all things are possible with God. In times of prosperity, strife, peace, and war, Americans lean on His infinite love, grace, and understanding. Let us come together and pray to the Almighty that through overcoming this coronavirus pandemic, we develop even greater faith in His divine providence.

In 1988, the Congress, by Public Law 100-307, as amended, called on the President to issue each year a proclamation designating the first Thursday in May as a National Day of Prayer, "on which the people of the United States may turn to God in prayer and meditation at churches, in groups, and as individuals."

NOW, THEREFORE, I, DONALD J. TRUMP, President of the United States of America, do hereby proclaim May 7, 2020, as a National Day of Prayer. I encourage all Americans to observe this day, reflecting on the blessings our Nation has received and the importance of prayer, with appropriate programs, ceremonies, and activities in their houses of worship, communities, and places of work, schools, and homes consistent with the White House's "Guidelines for Opening up America Again."

IN WITNESS WHEREOF, I have hereunto set my hand this sixth day of May, in the year of our Lord two thousand twenty, and of the Independence of the United States of America the two hundred and forty-fourth.

DONALD J. TRUMP [9]

One King and one Queen saved a nation. According to the scriptures, we are kings and queens being prepared to rule. [10]Who knows, maybe YOU were born for *Such A Time as This!*

MEET THE AUTHOR

JEFF JANSEN has authored six books: *Glory Rising: Walking in the Realm of Creative Miracles, Signs & Wonders; Glory Rising: Manual; Furious Sound of Glory; The Believers' Guide to Miracles, Healing, Impartation & Activation; Revival of the Secret Place*; and his latest book, *Enthroned*. He is also a contributing author to two books: *Adventures in the Prophetic*, along with James Goll, Patricia King, and others, and *Beyond 2012: What the Real Prophets are Saying*, with Bob Jones, Graham Cooke, and others.

Five Magnificent Books Written by Jeff Jansen

available at *Global Fire Ministries*

ENDNOTES

INTRODUCTION

1. Abraham Heschel, *The Prophets* (Harper Colins, New York, 2001) 287
2. Heschel, *The Prophets*, 568
3. Brueggemann, Walter, *The Prophetic Imagination* (Fortress Press, Minneapolis, 2018) 3
4. 2 Chronicles 7:14
5. Tony Evans, *If My People*, 2014, https://decisionmagazine.com/if-my-people/, Accessed August 1, 2020

1. LAND OF THE FREE AND HOME OF THE BRAVE

1. Newt Ginrich,Land of the Free and Home of the Brave https://www.gingrich360.com/2020/07/land-of-the-free-and-home-of-the-brave/, Accessed August 2, 2020
2. Ronald Raegan, Freedom Speech, https://www.reagan.com/ronald-reagan-freedom-speech#:~:text=Ronald%20Reagan%20Freedom%20Speech.%20August%2031%2C%202018%20PRIVA-CY,and%20after%20he%20was%20in%20the%20Oval%20Office., Accessed August 2, 2020

2. ANGEL OF LIBERTY

1. https://www.history.com/topics/american-revolution/valley-forge, Accessed August 6, 2020
2. https://www.ushistory.org/valleyforge/washington/vision.html, August 6, 2020
3. Account printed by National Tribute, in Washington, DC on December 2, 1880, https://chroniclingamerica.loc.gov/lccn/sn82016187/1880-12-01/ed-1/seq-1/, Accessed August 6, 2020

4. https://chroniclingamerica.loc.gov/data/batches/dlc_ike_ver01/data/
sn82016187/00211103516/18801201011/0256.pdf, Accessed August 6, 2020

5. Ibid, Accessed August 6, 2020, https://chroniclingamerica.loc.gov/data/
batches/dlc_ike_ver01/data/sn82016187/00211103516/18801201011/0256.pdf

6. From the Civil Liberties Website, http://www.timetobelieve.com/america/
prophecy-of-george-washington/, Accessed August 6, 2020

7. 2 Chronicles 7:14

8. *Psalm 33:12*

3. A FOUR HUNDRED YEAR DESTINY DOOR

1. See Philbrick, Nathaniel. *Mayflower: A Story of Courage, Community, and War*,(
Penguin Publishing, New York, 2006) ebook

2. See Marshall, Peter. *The Light and the Glory*, (Baker Publishing Group<
Minneapolis, 1977) p. 20

3. Ibid, Philbrick, Nathaniel. *Mayflower: A Story of Courage, Community, and War*

4. Ibid

5. Rev. E. W. Bishop, *The Pilgrim Forefathers*, *Lansing State Journal*, Michigan, Oct.
2, 1920) 4

6. https://www.history.com/topics/colonial-america/mayflower, Accessed
August 7, 2020

7. https://www.plimoth.org/learn/just-kids/homework-help/mayflower-and-
mayflower-compact, Accessed August 7, 2020

8. https://www.plimoth.org/learn/just-kids/homework-help/mayflower-and-
mayflower-compact, Accessed August 7, 2020

9. https://www.plimoth.org/learn/just-kids/homework-help/mayflower-and-
mayflower-compact. Accessed August 7, 2020

10. Lisa Rein, Mystery of Virginia's First Slaves, https://www.washingtonpost.com/
archive/politics/2006/09/03/mystery-of-vas-first-slaves-is-unlocked-400-years-
later/7015c871-aabd-4ba2-b5ce-7c0955aa0d75/, Accessed August 7, 2020

11. https://www.history.com/this-day-in-history/slavery-abolished-in-america,
Accessed August 7, 2020

12. https://www.history.com/topics/black-history/civil-rights-act, Accessed
August 7, 2020

13. For more see Susannah Heschel, Two Friends, Two Prophets, https://www.
plough.com/en/topics/community/leadership/two-friends-two-prophets,
Accessed August 7, 2020

14. Genesis 15:12-14

15. Exodus 9:1

16. 1 Corinthians 10:1-4

4. THE THIRD GREAT AWAKENING

1. https://www.myjewishlearning.com/article/judaism-numbers/,   Accessed August 8, 2020

5. THE TRUE HISTORY OF PRESIDENT DONALD J. TRUMP

1. https://www.politico.eu/article/the-tiny-scottish-village-that-spawned-trump/, Accessed August 9, 2020
2. See more at: https://earlybirdbooks.com/the-most-controversial-trump-biography, Accessed August 9, 2020
3. See more at: https://www.politico.com/magazine/story/2016/05/donald-trump-scottish-village-scotland-mother-213882, Accessed August 9, 2020
4. Dougherty, Steve (2016). "Family Saga". *Donald Trump: The Rise of a Rule Breaker*. Time Inc. Books.
5. Nic Robertson; Antonia Mortensen. "Donald Trump's Scottish roots". CNN. Retrieved November 6, 2017.
6. See more at: https://www.bbc.com/news/uk-scotland-38648877, Accessed August 9, 2020
7. See more at: https://sapphirethroneministries.wordpress.com/tag/mary-anne-smith-macleod-is-donald-trumps-mother/, Accessed August 9, 2020
8. See more at: https://welovetrump.com/2020/04/20/the-history-of-donald-trumps-bible/, Accessed August 9, 2020
9. https://womenofchristianity.com/the-intercessors-of-the-hebrides-revival-by-david-smithers/, August 9, 2020
10. https://freedomoutpost.com/religious-researchers-tie-donald-trump-to-hebrides-revival-in-scotland/, August 9, 2020
11. https://www.worldtribune.com/desperate-prayers-by-trumps-aunts-in-sanctuary-cottage-said-to-spark-hebrides-revival-in-scotland/,   Accessed August 9, 2020
12. See more at: https://www.stone-kingdom.net/blog/2020/04/president-trumps-scottish-bloodline-foreshadows-christian-revival, Accessed August 9, 2020
13. Article by Al Gibson, May 17, 2020, https://godtv.com/trumps-bible-has-historic-significance/, Accessed August 9, 2020

14. Article on Belief Net, https://www.beliefnet.com/prayers/christian/gratitude/billy-grahams-prayer-for-the-nation.aspx, Accessed August 9, 2020

6. CIVIL WAR IN AMERICA

1. For more see http://www.elijahlist.com/words/display_word.html?ID=10711, August 10, 202
2. A Single Garment of Destiny, https://alliesagainstslavery.org/blog-2016-1-18-a-single-garment-of-destiny/, August 10, 2020
3. 1 Corinthians 1:10
4. Mark Ross, https://www.ligonier.org/learn/articles/essentials-unity-non-essentials-liberty-all-things/, August 9, 2020
5. Barnes Commentary, https://biblehub.com/commentaries/1_corinthians/1-10.htm, Accessed August 10, 2020
6. Bretschneider, https://biblehub.com/commentaries/1_corinthians/1-10.htm, Accessed August 10, 2020
7. Barnes Commentary, https://biblehub.com/commentaries/1_corinthians/1-10.htm, Accessed August 10, 2020
8. 1 Corinthians 2:14
9. http://www.abrahamlincolnonline.org/lincoln/speeches/fast.htm, Accessed August 20, 2020

7. LADY LIBERTY'S FREEDOM TORCH

1. Ezekiel 44:23
2. *Malachi 3:1-3*, AMP
3. Malachi 3:16-18
4. *Malachi 4:1-6*
5. Donnie McClurkin, *Days of Elijah*, https://www.azlyrics.com/lyrics/donniemcclurkin/daysofelijah.html, Accessed August 10, 2020
6. *1 Kings 18:21*
7. Mark 9:2
8. John E. Thomas, *Where Are the Dread Champions*, https://streamsministries.com/where-are-the-dread-champions/, August 11, 2020
9. *Jeremiah 20:11*
10. https://blogs.timesofisrael.com/whos-crying-now/, August 11, 2020
11. Romans 8:31
12. https://www.angelalcraig.com/2019/07/lady-liberty/, August 11, 2020

8. THE LAST TRUMP, THE DESTINY OF GOD'S AMERICA

1. *1 Corinthians 15:52 AMP*
2. Uldis Sprogis, *Trump: An Unconventional Fighting President,* https://www.americanthinker.com/articles/2019/11/trump_an_unconventional_fighting_president.html, Accessed August 11, 2020
3. Newt Gingrich article, https://www.foxnews.com/opinion/trump-biden-2020-newt-gingrich, Accessed August 11, 2020
4. Ted Nugent, https://www.blabbermouth.net/news/ted-nugent-on-donald-trump-hes-on-a-mission-from-god-this-is-divine-intervention/, Accessed August 11, 2020
5. https://www.carolinacoastonline.com/news_times/opinions/letters_to_editor/article_bf740238-032f-11ea-822a-9ff3fdf6c7a3.html, August 11, 2020
6. http://www.leaderu.com/orgs/cdf/onug/madison.html, Accessed August 11, 2020
7. https://frcblog.com/2014/02/ronald-reagan-and-bible-rock-which-our-republic-rests/, August 11, 2020
8. Ibid.
9. *Mark 8:36*

9. FOR SUCH A TIME AS THIS

1. http://inotherwords.ac/what-are-you-saying/, Accessed August 4, 2020
2. https://michaelhyatt.com/words-changed-history/, Accessed August 5, 2020
3. http://www.gettysburg.com/bog/address.htm, Accessed August 5, 2020
4. 2 Kings 19:15-19
5. 2 Kings 19:32, 34
6. Refer to https://jentezenfranklin.org/fast/fasting-that-changed-history-part-2, Accessed August 5, 2020
7. Esther 4:14
8. Joel 1:14
9. Proclamation on National Day of Prayer, 2020, https://www.whitehouse.gov/presidential-actions/proclamation-national-day-prayer-2020/, Accessed August 5, 2020
10. 1 Corinthians 6:2, 3

CPSIA information can be obtained
at www.ICGtesting.com
Printed in the USA
LVHW020056190121
676853LV00012B/258